USING TRAINING AIDS IN TRAINING AND DEVELOPMENT

A practical guide for trainers and presenters

USING TRAINING AIDS IN TRAINING AND DEVELOPMENT

A practical guide for trainers and presenters

Leslie Rae

KOGAN
PAGE

London • Sterling (USA)

YOURS TO HAVE AND TO HOLD

BUT NOT TO COPY

First published in 1998

Apart from any fair dealing for the purposes of research or private study, or criticism or review, as permitted under the Copyright, Designs and Patents Act 1988, this publication may only be reproduced, stored or transmitted, in any form or by any means, with the prior permission in writing of the publishers, or in the case of reprographic reproduction in accordance with the terms and licences issued by the CLA. Enquiries concerning reproduction outside those terms should be sent to the publishers at the undermentioned address:

Kogan Page Limited
120 Pentonville Road
London N1 9JN, UK
and
Stylus Publishing Inc.
22883 Quicksilver Drive
Sterling, VA 20166, USA

© Leslie Rae, 1998

The right of Leslie Rae to be identified as author of this work has been asserted by him in accordance with the Copyright, Designs and Patents Act 1988.

British Library Cataloguing in Publication Data

A CIP record for this book is available from the British Library.

ISBN 0 7494 2806 6

Typeset by JS Typesetting, Wellingborough, Northants
Printed and bound in Great Britain by Biddles Ltd, Guildford and King's Lynn

Contents

Preface

> ## PURPOSES OF THIS BOOK
>
> The purposes of this book are:
>
> ◆ to describe the use of aids in training and development
>
> ◆ to encourage their use

The purposes of this book are to describe the use of aids in training and development and to encourage their use.

I have started this book in this way to try to demonstrate the impact that aids, particularly visual ones, have on presentations. The two text lines below the box restate in normal book form the message presented in the box. Which approach made more impact on you and gave you the most immediate information about the message? I hope your answer is 'the boxed statement'! But I feel I am on fairly safe ground, as the box represents a typical visual aid poster. The differences between it and the text message are the same as those between the spoken word and visual aids in a verbal presentation.

The book is about the use of training aids, designed for use by:

- trainers in the design and production of training events
- managers and coaches who undertake training and development in addition to their line duties and need the support of comprehensive and easily understood support material
- presenters and others who want (or need) to enhance their oral presentations; and by individuals who are on a self-instruction path.

The value of visual aids in particular was described many years ago by Confucius (or was attributed to him) and part of his learning statement is:

Preface

I hear and I forget
I see and I remember.

The last line, not reproduced above, reads *'I do and I understand'*, completing one of the basic messages on learning for trainers. However, here we are concentrating on the 'see' part of presentation, which at least takes learning one step further than the passive act of hearing.

Learning does not just happen. Something else has to be involved to ensure that it does. This 'something' is the act of learning, via training and development events from a wide variety of forms, the exact format depending on the situation. 'Learning' is the act of the person who has to develop some aspect of knowledge, skill or attitude; 'training' is the action taken to help that learning be achieved. In both these activities, training aids have a major part to play in ensuring the achievement of learning.

The training session, input session, lecture and presentation in communication and training and development have specific objectives of giving and receiving, exchanging and sharing information, knowledge, views and opinions in order to develop the knowledge levels of the learners in the trinity of knowledge, skills and attitudes. Sessions can rarely, and are not intended to, develop skills; only practical activity and application, artificial or real, can do this. But before skill can develop, the knowledge base must exist, either learned fully or developed in the training session. Skill can appear with no element of learning input, but it will almost always be an extended process, faltering, painful, costly and frequently dangerous. Training sessions can be developed into fully effective learning events by extending them from the usually ineffective 'tell' alone events, to ones with impact, interest, variety and enjoyment – all elements that assist learning – by the use of training aids.

Visual presentation alone has taken tremendous strides since the days of the first aid in general use, the universal blackboard from the school classroom, although there is still a significant place for simple aids such as this, or its modern counterpart, the whiteboard. Audio and visual aids have also taken substantial steps from the early days of the film and audio cassette recorder disturbing the peace of the training room. The sections of this book will present most of the aids available to trainers and other presenters.

Pictures, drawings and other graphic images brighten and uplift our daily lives – even an art-illiterate person responds to the most common visual aid of the present day, the television image. Training sessions and presentations can be (and frequently are) boring and forgettable occasions without some image to enliven the spoken word, but can undergo a remarkable change with effective aids, even of the simplest nature.

Learners present a greater challenge to trainers (of whatever nature) than ever before. Their exposure to 'professional' presenters, radical techniques and a variety of images through television and computers raises their expectations of any training event they attend, and poor presentation can have a serious effect on their learning – and we fail in our intent. Learning does not *have* to be an enjoyable experience, but the majority of people learn more quickly, more easily and with lasting consequences if it is enjoyable as well as effective in other ways.

COPYRIGHT

When you are developing any type of learning or training aid that involves using somebody else's material – text, images or photographs, sound recordings, videos, music, or computer programs – you must always seek copyright permission. This is relevant whether you intend to use even small sections of text or parts of the graphics, etc. Granting of copyright permission can be expensive, but so can the penalties under the legislation! In many cases, however, in my experience, publishers and authors make no charge for reproduction provided full credit is given to the source, since this is a form of advertising for them. Some books (usually collections of training activities) give a blanket authority to copy material, provided this is done and used by the purchaser of the publication.

Copyright is covered in the UK by the Copyright, Designs and Patents Act 1988, and incorporates not just books but videos, sound recordings, films, music, photographs, CD-I and computer programs.

Copyright legislation is a very complex subject, and where there is any question of its possible infringement you should always approach the copyright owner or, in important and complex cases, a lawyer who specializes in this area.

However, useful points to bear in mind include the following.

- UK copyright law covers works by British citizens, and works published in the UK and certain places elsewhere.
- The UK has signed international conventions that bestow the same protection both to foreign copyright holders in the UK and to UK nationals overseas (various countries have different copyright protections that must also be considered).

- In general copyright is protected for 50 years after the author's death, or 125 years from creation in the case of a Crown copyright.
- Copying of less than a 'substantial' part of the work may not infringe copyright – unfortunately there is no definition of 'substantial', this depending not only on length, but also importance.
- Research and private study for personal use only is not an infringement.
- Reading to an audience is permitted.
- Educational establishments are allowed to copy material for examinations and instruction, the latter under specific restrictions.
- There is no copyright on ideas provided these are reworked and rephrased and give due acknowledgement to the source.
- A number of publishers of training material permit copying of material by the purchaser for use in the purchaser's organization.

Format

The book is structured in a reasonably logical and progressive format, starting with the reasoning behind the use of training and learning aids, then describing the more commonly used aids, the more recent innovations of a technical nature, and the wider aspects. The intention has been to make the content as practical and as usable as possible and checklists, summaries and examples should help in this process. The instruments are suggestions only and most can be easily modified to suit individual circumstances.

Acknowledgements

I should like to thank the following organization for its courtesy, help and kind permission to reproduce clip-art images from its products for use as graphic illustrations: Serif Inc (Serif PagePlus Home/Office Edition and Serif Mega ArtPack CD-ROM) for all clip-art graphic illustrations.

I should also thank Philip Mudd and Will Mackie of Kogan Page Ltd for their valuable support and advice, and Jacqueline Twyman of First Impressions for her valuable support in ensuring that many deficiencies in the manuscript were avoided (I must still accept responsibility for the end result).

W Leslie Rae

Learning and Communication

The purposes of a presentation, whether it is part of a training programme or a specific presentation, are to inform in an effective way or to induce learning in the participants. Both the practitioner and the learner must welcome any techniques or methods that can support or even enhance these purposes.

THE COMPETENCE STEPLADDER

Learning is the process of change and can be demonstrated by the competence steps shown in Figure 1.1.

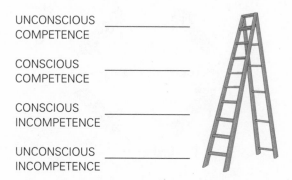

UNCONSCIOUS
COMPETENCE

CONSCIOUS
COMPETENCE

CONSCIOUS
INCOMPETENCE

UNCONSCIOUS
INCOMPETENCE

Figure 1.1 *The competence stepladder*

People performing a task or role may be doing so without complete competence; but they are unaware of these deficiencies, until by a variety of mechanisms they may be made aware of these and so pass up the steps to the area of conscious incompetence. As a result of taking some learning action they become capable and competent in the process, but have to perform it consciously and deliberately. Full implementation, practice and performance at work raises the level to the top step of unconscious competence, where learning has been achieved and the task is performed effectively without too much thought. A problem is that, all too easily, unconscious competence can slip back to unconscious incompetence!

Learning programmes set out to achieve this change, at least to the borderline between conscious and unconscious competence, but this learning needs to be achieved in a variety of ways, and with a number of resources.

THE LEARNING INVENTORY

As the result of extensive research and observation of practices, it is generally accepted that every individual learner is different and learns in a different way although there are specific groups with similar learning characteristics. The approach was pioneered by Kolb in the 1970s in the US and by Honey and Mumford (1982) in the UK, among others, and shows that effective learning is achieved by using all four stages of the *Learning Cycle* shown diagramatically as Figure 1.2.

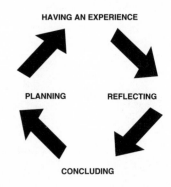

Figure 1.2 *The Learning Cycle*

In this cycle the learners start by experiencing something – an event, a feeling, a statement, etc – and, instead of moving on, as so frequently happens, to the next experience, the individual stops to reflect on all the aspects of *what* happened. This consideration is then taken further to conclude *why* it happened, whether it could have been performed in another (better) way, and what theories or models underpin the event. The final action, when the foregoing have been considered and learning has taken place from this consideration, is to use this learning in a repeat of the event or in planning another event.

LEARNING PREFERENCES

Unfortunately not everybody follows this cycle when learning opportunities are presented, many becoming locked in at one stage or another, and as a consequence the full range of learning is inhibited. Honey and Mumford demonstrated that people have learning preferences in one or more of the four areas: some simply experience something and pass on to the next event, learning little or nothing as a result; others are locked in on the reflective stage, preferring to sit and think about activities rather than take some form of action and then learning by reflection; yet others theorize endlessly and become so locked into the intricacies of the models that they rarely move on to actually doing something. Yet others are so bound up in the interesting intricacies of planning what to do that they either do not get around to putting the plan into action or, if they do, circumstances change and negate their plans with the result that they are devastated.

This 'locking in' has obvious detrimental effects on learning and can be one of the major barriers. If a training programme is presented in the theorist mode, the presenter expounding theories, models and concepts in a continuous stream, with little opportunity for the 'learners' to reflect on them or try them out, the theorists in the group are more likely to learn at the expense of little or no learning by those with other preferences. More effective learning can be achieved by affording time between models for reflection (perhaps guided for those for whom this is not a natural process!) and opportunities provided for the learners to experiment or implement the theories. If the explanations are supported by training aids, the learning is likely to be even more effective.

By means of these relatively simple modifications to what used to be a common approach – the straight lecture – learning can become an enjoyable event, even though those who are locked in on a particular approach will not enjoy the time spent on the preferred approaches of others. The trite saying that 'you can't please all the people all the time' is so true in training and development! Figure 1.3 summarizes these learning preferences.

THE ACTIVIST – PREFERS AND NEEDS TO BE *DOING* SOMETHING (ANYTHING?)

THE REFLECTOR – PREFERS TO SIT AND CONSIDER WHAT HAS HAPPENED, BY WHOM, TO WHOM (PERHAPS RATHER THAN ACTUALLY *DOING* IT)

THE THEORIST – PREFERS TO CONSIDER THE CONCEPTS AND THEORIES BEHIND WHAT HAPPENED, MODELS OF ACTIVITY AND ALTERNATIVES

THE PRAGMATIST – HAS IT A PRACTICAL APPLICATION? IS IT WORTH DOING? HOW CAN I APPLY IT BACK AT WORK? IF NONE OF THESE APPLY, I'M NOT INTERESTED

Figure 1.3 *The Learning Preferences*

SENSORY LEARNING

Additional to the learning preferences can be the reactions of learners to and their ability to learn from sensory effects – hearing, seeing, touching, smelling, visualizing, doing, and so on. People's sensory preference can often be identified by their verbal responses to communication from others. The person who prefers to be given information orally may respond 'I *hear* what you are saying'. The person who prefers to see learning approaches, eg graphic visual aids during a talk, will comment 'Yes, I *see* what you mean'. Consequently, in the same way that we found people had learning preferences, sensory preferences can also have a significant effect on how and how much they learn. These senses are summarized in Figure 1.4 and then described in more detail.

SIGHT
Learning by reading   Learning by seeing
Learning by visualization   Learning by writing
Hearing
Learning by listening

TOUCH
Learning by touching (objects, machines, people)
Learning by the experience of doing

SMELL/TASTE
Learning by smelling or tasting products, situations, environments and so on.

Figure 1.4 *The use of the senses in learning*

The sense of sight

Sensory learning includes four preferences that rely on the sense of sight:

- *Learning by reading.* This learning preference can be translated into reading information, skill techniques or procedural written material. It is an approach that can be difficult for many and is fraught with problems caused by the level of intellect, understanding capabilities and other considerations such as language, particularly where a number of races and cultures might be involved. Reflectors and theorists are usually more at home in this medium. There is little doubt that when the words are accompanied by pictures the acceptance of the words is supported. However, this is not an easy or cheap addition to the pages of most books that are dominated by text.
- *Learning by seeing.* Many people have to see something before they can understand and, as a result, learn. The sight might be the object itself, a model, or even a graphic visual aid or computer graphic. Seeing the object of learning avoids the necessity of the learners' attempting to visualize. Use of such objects should be easily introduced in most, if not all, learning events.
- *Learning by visualization.* This is a difficult approach that requires the learners, from verbal or written descriptions, to visualize an

object, event or concept. Frequently this approach is used in conjunction with sight of the item after a visualizing description has been made to prepare the learners.

■ *Learning by writing.* Whether it is the act of copying something from an existing text; interpreting, analysing and summarizing an extended text; or making notes from a verbal presentation, many people find the act of writing something down helps their learning, retention and recall.

The sense of hearing

The sense of hearing can have a significant effect on learning.

■ *Learning by listening.* Those who find it difficult to learn via the written word, whether it is through difficulties of understanding or an inherent problem with the medium, will frequently understand and learn from the spoken word. This approach to learning usually takes place in an environment where questioning and discussion can take place, thus helping the learning process.

The sense of touch

Although somewhat more limited, the sense of touch cannot be ignored in encouraging effective learning and, in particular, if it is considered in terms of *doing*, it can then become the most important of all.

■ *Learning by touching.* As already stated touching has a more limited, but none the less significant application in the learning of certain skills, particularly for those where a few minutes of hands-on experience is worth hours of description. In the training environment the opportunity to 'have a go' can avoid many problems if the first practice is to be in the real world of work – try to describe the feel of a snake's skin if neither you nor the learner has previously held a snake.

■ *Learning by doing.* This approach is considered by many as the ultimate in learning processes, usually preceded by other forms such as verbal descriptions and graphical representations. The learners are given the opportunity, usually under supervision or observation, to perform an act, whether it is practically operational, procedural or one requiring the performance of task or people skills.

The senses of smell and taste

The final sense, that of smell and taste is perhaps even more limited in application, but in specific forms of training must be considered as an aid to learning. If the training of gas meter readers ignores the opportunity for them to actually smell escaping gas, this training is not as effective as it should be, particularly if the learners have lived in an all-electric environment and have never smelled domestic gas. Similarly, learner perfume practitioners have an essential need for the effective use of this sense.

The ideal learning environment must, therefore, be one in which the training makes use of as many of the sensory tools as are relevant and available, recognizing (as with the learning preferences of Honey and Mumford) that the locked-in sensory preferences of some people may have a significant effect on the learning. My sense of smell is so limited that this approach would not appeal to me; a trainee electrician failed early in his training when it became apparent that he had colour deficiencies in his sight; other 'disabilities', major and minor, can all contribute to barriers to learning.

Whatever the sensory and other learning preference approach, it must be that the more varied the training approach the more the senses are stimulated. The more the learners will learn. A training programme or presentation including the variety of approaches shown in Figure 1.5 has a much greater likelihood of producing real learning than one with very restricted approaches.

■ VERBAL INPUT SESSIONS
  WITH SUPPORTING AIDS,
  VISUAL AND AUDITORY
■ PRACTICAL ACTIVITIES
■ THEORETICAL DISCUSSION
■ TIME FOR REFLECTION
■ TIME FOR PRAGMATIC
  FORWARD PLANNING

Figure 1.5 *A varied training programme*

A COMMUNICATION MODEL

In any communication there is a sender and a receiver, and all communication would be effective if these were the only factors involved. Unfortunately this is not so. Figure 1.6a illustrates graphically the bases of the problems; Figure 1.6b shows the extension of the problems when the presentation is being made to a number of people, such as a training group or presentation audience.

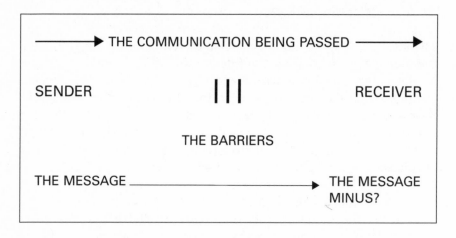

Figure 1.6a *The one-to-one communication model*

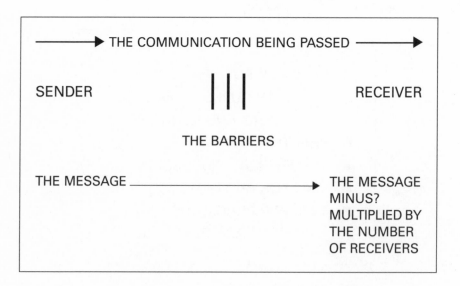

Figure 1.6b *The group communication model*

Figure 1.6a shows that between the sending of the message and its reception there can be a number of barriers. These barriers can be erected by either the sender or the receiver – usually by both – and in the case of *one* receiver can vary depending on the individual on each occasion. One sender and one receiver can erect certain barriers; another sender and receiver a different set of barriers. And of course one common sender can find different barriers with different receivers, demanding recognition of the barriers in each case. The sender can be the principal person erecting the barriers to the successful passage of the communication, and unfortunately may not be aware of this. We have seen earlier how differing styles of presenters can produce various barriers.

The problem is exacerbated, as shown in Figure 1.6b, when the receivers are a group of individuals. Many of these may have the same barriers, but it is likely that each individual will also have his or her own set!

Effective presentation is *your* surmounting as many of these barriers as possible. You must recognize your own barriers and those of the audience members and attempt to do something about them. This process is obviously easier for you and your own problems, once recognized, but it is much more difficult to overcome those of the audience.

BARRIERS TO VERBAL COMMUNICATION

If you are to be effective or increase your effectiveness as a presenter you must be able to recognize the barriers to successful communication and work out strategies to try to overcome them. These barriers can be identified within four main groups – speech (such as the use of jargon), internal or psychological aspects (such as mood), non-verbal aspects (such as stance), and environmental (such as temperature). Some of these relate to you, others to the audience, others to both you and the audience, and still others to external circumstances. Breaking down the barriers by using training aids will not always be successful, but their use will considerably increase the likelihood in the majority of cases. Part of *your* barriers might be the problems of identifying which approach and aids will be the most successful.

SPECIFIC BARRIERS

Figure 1.7 summarizes the principal barriers encountered; these are then described in more detail.

SPEECH
Vocabulary   Jargon
Woolly approach and/or rambling   Unusual words
Lack of speaking skill   Accent
Lack of knowledge

INTERNAL OR PSYCHOLOGICAL ASPECTS
Pressures   Mood
Forced resistance   Fear
Shyness   Aggression
Resistance to learning and change   Know-it-all
Too old to learn or change   Status differences

NON-VERBAL ASPECTS
Manner   Attitude:
                                          prejudicial
                                          judgemental
                                          over directive

THE ENVIRONMENT
Noise. Heat. Cold. Ventilation.
Space available. Interruptions/Work intrusion
Restricted time

Figure 1.7   *Barriers to effective listening*

Speech

Most of the barriers caused by speech are the result of the presenter's delivery, and most are capable of rectification.

Vocabulary. The vocabulary must be within the listeners' range of understanding, otherwise you might as well be talking in a foreign language!

Jargon. It is so easy to pick up the jargon of the organization or the discipline, but if the listeners do not come from the same environment the jargon will not only not be understood, it will annoy.

Ambiguity. Be careful that you say what you mean, not simply what you mean to say. Extra care is essential when multicultures form the audience, in view of differing meanings to some words and sayings.

Woolly approach and/or rambling. Keep KISS (Keep It Short and Simple) in mind and the long, vague rambling speech will be avoided. Otherwise the audience may well stop listening or even fall asleep.

Unusual words. If the words are unfamiliar to you, ensure that you are using the best word, the right word, and that you are pronouncing it correctly. Are you using it because it is the best/only/correct/most appropriate word, or are you simply using it for effect? Is the audience likely to understand it?

Lack of speaking skill. An unskilled speaker will use methods and techniques that are not the most effective with which to make an impact on the listeners. Too many hesitations, verbal noises, mannerisms and so on will be noted by the listeners, who may take more notice of these than of what is being said. There may be an element of sympathy for the inexperienced speaker, but lack of skill is unlikely to be approved of.

Accent. At one time regional accents were not acceptable for many areas of public speaking. This is no longer the case, but if the accent is too strong it may not be understandable. The use of dialect words should, however, be avoided as these may not be widely understood.

Lack of knowledge. The converse of knowing it all and letting everybody know this is demonstrating that the speaker's knowledge of the subject is limited or incomplete. The listener, particularly in a learning situation, has every justification in rejecting someone who has obviously not taken sufficient care in preparation in order to know the subject. Naturally not everybody knows everything and at times the speaker will admit to some lack of knowledge, making a firm promise to find out the answer. But if this becomes an over-frequent admission credibility will soon be lost.

The know-it-all. You may be an expert on the subject and may in fact know 'all' there is to know about it, but listeners are very easily turned off by someone who ensures that they become aware of this vast extent of knowledge.

The support of training aids

Many of the barriers concerning speech can be lowered to a lesser or greater extent, or in some cases demolished altogether if the spoken word is supported by some form of aid, most often a visual aid – OHP slide, flipchart sheet or whiteboard entry. Obviously no aid can replace all the spoken words (many of which may be causing the barrier), but if the speech barrier cannot be modified at least the learners have something with which to refer to in their puzzlement.

Remember that the most effective training aid, if properly and effectively used, is *yourself*, and the learners are using you as their reference point in the same way that a projected OHP slide becomes their point of major attention.

Internal or psychological aspects

Pressures. All sorts of pressures are on members of an audience and these can detract from what you say and distract their attention – work, health, domestic, money, learning, social, etc pressures can all have an effect. A member of the audience who is waiting to hear the results of medical tests on themselves or their partner, or is in the process of having a difficult house move, is not likely to be listening to you completely.

Mood. The listener who is easily affected by moods may be in such a mood during your presentation that listening to you may not be a priority. Similarly, you can have moods or be affected by situations that cause your mind to be not completely on your presentation: this will certainly affect your presentation and the way it is received.

Forced resistance. Not every member of the audience attends a presentation voluntarily, and when made to attend they are most unlikely to be in a receptive mood and will, perhaps, actively resist change. In the same way, some presenters are unwilling contributors – they may have been given a three-line whip to give the talk and this will have an effect, particularly if other factors relating to the subject enter into the equation.

Fear. Fear can be a strong motivator for listening and learning, but if it is too strong it becomes a barrier, the fear being uppermost in the person's mind. We will be returning later to the subject of the *presenter's* fears and the effects – suffice to say here that it can obviously have some effect on the presentation.

Shyness. Any member of the audience has overcome the first shyness barrier by actually attending, but if something is not understood the shyness may prevent a question, with the result that what follows is lost. Extreme shyness on the part of the presenter will have an effect on the speech, with a too quiet, too hesitant, confused presentation resulting.

Aggression. This may be linked with enforced attendance, an on-the-spot dislike of you, the environment or the other members, and it will usually exhibit itself by an aggressive expression which is developed rather than listening to what you are saying, or sometimes even by a vocal attack on you. If for some reason you as the presenter are feeling aggressive – not necessarily towards the audience – this will show in your delivery. Remember that behaviour breeds behaviour and the audience may react to your aggression with a similar attitude.

Resistance to learning and change. There can be many reasons for this attitude – enforced attendance, failure to see the reason for the presentation, various dislikes and so on. 'I do not intend to learn/listen/change, etc' can sometimes be broken down by involvement or an interesting presentation or activity, but often it stays throughout the session.

Know-it-all. This is one of the most common resistances to learning, particularly by any long-serving employee who has been sent to the presentation against their wishes. If this is the case it is more effective to try to use their experience within the group than to react against the attitude.

Too old to learn or change. This is usually an attitude developed by those who are frightened to learn or who for some other reason do not want to learn. Research has shown however that, unless older people have allowed their minds to degenerate, they are often, because of a wealth of experience, better learners than many younger people.

Status differences. If the audience members are at different status levels within the organization, unless the group is well established, the higher level members may resist in case they make fools of themselves in front of their juniors, who themselves do not want to take the risk of showing themselves up in front of their bosses.

The support of training aids

When internal or psychological barriers are present training aids can do little directly. The principal agent for lowering these forms of barrier must be you, the trainer or presenter, making your contribution so interesting and obviously important to the members, that they are able to cast aside their internal problem constructs. The use of training aids will provide variety, interest and points of focus to support your presentation and help to raise their interest level.

Non-verbal aspects

Non-verbal aspects of speech and other non-verbal communication are very extensive subjects and there are many relevant books and videos that give complete descriptions and explanations. Too much can sometimes be read into the effects of non-verbal aspects, but you must be aware of them. Perhaps the principal consideration must be whether or not whatever you are doing non-verbally is having a detrimental effect on your presentation. If your non-verbal gestures or mannerisms are so excessive that the audience is watching for these rather than listening to the presentation, then they are interfering and you should modify them. But many of these mannerisms are 'us' and help to humanize us instead of our being impersonal presenters – but we must be careful not to overdo them. Two aspects that may be exhibited non-verbally during a presentation concern your overt manner and the overt expression of your attitude.

Manner. Speakers may not be able to control completely their integral manner, but usually this can be modified somewhat for the period required. A patronizing manner is soon recognized and rejected by the listeners; aggression from the speaker results in either withdrawal or returned aggression – neither of which are conducive to good communication; an abrasive manner has a similar effect. Speakers can usually modify the first two; the last one is more difficult as the speaker may not even be aware of this aspect of his or her natural manner.

Attitude. This is often an aspect that speakers do not recognize in themselves, but which nevertheless may have an effect on the extent of listening and acceptance. The speaker's **prejudices** may emerge unconsciously – racism, sexism and so on, and even personal views that ignore or reject the views of others without reason or argument. The speaker may be **judgemental**, making decisions or forcing opinions without seeking other options, and, perhaps because of these two aspects and other internal motivation, may be **over directive**. You have to be completely aware of these possible attitudes in yourself (if you are not sure, ask a friend or colleague, or your partner) and, if they are present, modify your approach accordingly.

The support of training aids

The use of training aids in this area can be very productive because visual aids are themselves non-verbal communications, and if they are offered with a positive verbal accompaniment they can make a significant mark on the learning. Some of this will depend on the apparent value of the aid – currency, clarity, care, customization – and other effects will result from the use of the aid. Is it used with an apologetic manner or put forward positively; referred to almost as if it was not necessary or as the valuable support it is; used in a slapdash manner or used as a professional product by a professional user?

The environment

Noise. Heat. Cold. Ventilation. Space available. These are all aspects of the environment that can get in the way of listening and learning, as they all impinge on the various senses. Sometimes they can be resolved and the barrier is broken; at other times nothing can be done and they may remain as barriers which must be accepted as such.

Interruptions/Work intrusion. Interruptions of whatever nature, but particularly if they bring work into the environment, will affect listening and learning. Most can be avoided by taking preliminary precautions.

Restricted time. Learning and change of attitude and process require a variable length of time to be effective – time to fit in the material of the event; time for different people to assimilate material; time for you to put over the material effectively; and so on. Any time restriction will have a detrimental effect on both you and the listener.

The support of training aids

In all the barriers described the absence of training aids, although not destroying the presentation, will certainly reduce its effect and impact, because with their use more of the learners' senses are being encouraged to link the various aspects of the training into effective learning. Training aids will not ensure the full success of a presentation, particularly an intrinsically poor one, but they will certainly enhance the moderate presentation and lift the good one to satisfying heights, with the knowledge that everything feasible has been done to support the participants in their learning process.

THE LEARNING ATTENTION SPAN

All or some of the barriers described can contribute to the major barrier presented to a trainer or presenter – the length of listeners' effective attention time. Any group has a natural limited attention span that can be reduced even further by the presence of some of the barriers described above. This attention span can obviously be affected by many factors – for example the skill or charisma of the presenter, the subject interest, the need to learn, the attitude of the learners – but few groups will continue with maximum attention for the whole of, say, a 45 minutes input session. In general, attention starts to wander only a few minutes after the start of the session and continues to reduce until about the 20 minutes point when, unless something is done, the session impact, and hence learning, will be lost.

If at all possible, just before the 20 minute watershed (or earlier if inattention is becoming evident) vary the pace or form of the input to produce a major or minor attention jolt. You should repeat this injection at subsequent intervals, shorter than 20 minutes, to maintain the attention.

Training aids can play a major role in preventing this potential failure of communication. They can quite naturally break the simple flow of the speaker's presentation by changing its tone, speed and format. Even the displaying of an aid produces a short break and the aid itself will introduce a further reduction in the lack of attention. Obviously the aid must not be used only for this purpose, but must be relevant to the session itself, otherwise it could have a negative effect. Similarly, the use of too many aids in one session can produce a reaction against the event, the aids replacing the continuous voice of the presenter.

Obviously the '20-minute rule' will not apply to every presentation. Factors that can also vary the format will include the skills and possibly the charisma of the speaker; the need to learn; the interest and/or value of the subject matter; whether the session is mid-morning, immediately pre-lunch or post-lunch, or the last session of the day. The wise presenter will be prepared for and alert to any indications of reducing attention, and will take out an appropriate technique from the trainer's toolkit.

One common occurrence is an apparent slight upturn of interest shortly before the end of the session – the learners are not really listening more effectively, they are simply aware that the session has only a short while to go before it ends!

2
—

Choosing Training and Learning Aids

In some respects placing this chapter at this point is rather like putting the cart before the horse – if you don't know the qualities of the individual training aids, how do you know which one to use? But the material may at least point you to aids that might suit your purpose rather than your having to consider everything (a time-consuming process) and you can bear your requirements in mind as you research the various aids.

THE NEED FOR TRAINING AIDS

The previous chapter described the many barriers to learning that exist. The basic purpose of a training aid is to support the trainer or presenter, by ensuring that their verbal presentation is as acceptable as possible with a maximum of ensuing learning. The benefits offered by training aids include the following.

- VARIETY AND RETENTION
- GREATER IMPACT
- RECALL REINFORCEMENT
- AN AID TO CLARITY AND CONCISENESS
- CONSISTENCY AND QUALITY OF THOUGHT

Variety

The spoken word alone, even with the most charismatic speaker, soon loses its impact and, as we saw in the previous section, very early in a presentation there needs to be something to reawaken interest and maintain attention. Visual aids in particular offer sufficient variety from the spoken word to do this. In addition, most people are able to accept and remember more learning presented to them visually than verbally alone. Much of our memory relies on 'photographic' images and the visual aid offers exactly these, particularly as it will usually be associated with the trainer's words.

Greater impact

In addition to introducing variety to a presentation or session, a training aid can have more impact than the trainer's words alone. As suggested above, we are more likely to take notice of words linked with an image than words alone. If the image is very different or otherwise striking acceptance of the learning may be even greater. There are innumerable ways of introducing impact to an aid, particularly a visual one, often by giving a new angle to a familiar object. I have seen this demonstrated by the hands of a clock moving anticlockwise, or a clock with the 12 at the bottom instead of the top and the other figures in their different relative positions. These changes make the observer take more notice of the image than the otherwise immediate acceptance of an image with which you are familiar. This introduces impact and the likelihood of increased learning.

Recall reinforcement

The approaches just described help learners not only to learn, but also recall more and with greater ease at a later stage. Verbally we try to do this on many occasions by:

- TELLING PEOPLE WHAT WE ARE GOING TO TELL THEM
- TELLING THEM
- TELLING THEM WHAT WE HAVE TOLD THEM

These are the general principles of repetition and impact. The training aid guides the learner through this verbal jungle, pointing visually the direction in which the session is heading, or telling them where it has been.

Aid to clarity and conciseness

A picture or an object can say simply and quickly what it would take many words to explain, with no guarantee of understanding. We have looked at the senses of hearing, seeing, touching and smelling; a visual aid format such as that shown in Figure 2.1 could be used to reinforce a verbal description.

Figure 2.1   *Graphic representations of some of the learning senses*

Consistency and quality of thought

Training aids that are prepared for a session or presentation need to be thought out well in advance so that, linked with the words that will be spoken, they become considered objects rather than top-of-the-head scribblings. We know how much impact they are going to make and want this impact to be positive. I have certainly had the experience of starting to produce a visual aid only to realize that the entry in my session brief was either incomplete or incorrect. Once an effective aid is produced it can be used on each relevant occasion, so ensuring that the message given to different groups is consistent one with the other and with the original objective.

AVAILABLE AIDS

The training aids that are in use today are listed below, the more common ones annotated with a ✳ or ✳✳ (for very common use) and ■ or ■■ (for very rare use):

```
✳✳   ACTIVITIES
✳/■   CHALKBOARDS
■■   COMBINED AUDIO AND SLIDE PRESENTERS
✳/■   COMPUTERS
✳✳   FLIPCHARTS
■■   EPISCOPES
✳✳   HANDOUTS
■    INTERACTIVE VIDEOS
✳✳   OVERHEAD PROJECTORS
✳    SLIDE PROJECTORS
✳    THE OBJECT
✳    TRAINERS THEMSELVES (ALBEIT UNWITTINGLY)
✳✳   VIDEOS
■    VIDEO PROJECTORS
✳✳   WHITEBOARDS
```

THE SELECTION PROCESS

You may, of course, not have the luxury of choosing the aid(s) you prefer or need because of availability, but as will be seen later some aids are more suited to particular forms of event than others, and if possible the choice should be made on this basis.

Questions to ask

- What am I trying to achieve in this session or presentation? What are its objectives?
- Can the session objectives be achieved without training aids?
- Even though the objectives can be achieved without aids, will learning be made easier and/or improved if the verbal presentation is supported?
- Do the session objectives, content and style demand the support of training aids?

- Will training aids improve the presentation?
- Which aids will be the most appropriate?
- How many will I need?
- Is it feasible to use the number on which I decide?
- Have I the resources – time, staff support, finance – to produce or obtain the aids?

Session objectives

The objectives you have set for your session or presentation can have an effect on the use of training aids during the event, always bearing in mind the caveat on a learning group's attention span described in the previous chapter. The critical question you will need to ask is 'What type of event will be most effective to achieve its objectives and what support to the verbal presentation will be necessary?' If the presentation is short, with a simple message, there may be no need for any visual aid, or perhaps only the simplest, putting the message into a visual form. On the other hand some sessions will contain so much complex material that it would be foolhardy to rely on the spoken word alone – it may be that several media might be necessary to achieve the session objectives: flipchart, OHP, videos, computer program, detailed hand-outs and so on. This might appear to go against the initial advice of not including too many aids in one session, but the number must be balanced against the need to clarify the message.

Sessions involving the learning of practical skills with the physical objects or scale models being available are obvious situations for appeal to the senses of sight and touch (perhaps smell) in addition to verbal approaches.

In most cases, unless there are special circumstances, you will decide on the necessary use of training aids, so you can then continue to consider in specific terms the aids you would use.

The most appropriate aids

The most appropriate aids will depend, as suggested above, on the nature of the session or presentation and the type of aid(s) that will support the overall approach to the greatest extent. The aids to include in some training approaches are almost self-evident, whereas in others there can be difficulty in deciding whether to use aids and, if so, which ones.

The training approaches for which you may consider using training aids include:

- Activities
- Case studies
- Computer-based training
- Demonstrations
- Group discussions
- Input sessions
- Interactive video
- One-to-one instruction
- Presentations
- Projects
- Role plays

If your training event is to include one or more of the above approaches you will need to decide for each whether training aids will enhance the event. Two aspects of the approach need to be considered in detail to enable this decision to be made:

1. the characteristics of the approach
2. relevant training aids.

If we take as an example a demonstration training event of the operation of a physical task in which some machinery or other equipment is used, a summary of the considerations would include the following.

Characteristics

A demonstration is usually a practical, skills training approach that is frequently part of the tell–show–do technique in which, first, the skill is presented in an input session, which has its own selection of training aids. The trainer then shows or demonstrates the skill operation by a range of methods, and finally the learners take part in an activity in which they have hands-on experience, with evaluation or assessment of their performance against the session objectives.

The 'show' or demonstration part of the session must give the learners a clear representation of the operation or service and evidence of the skills required.

The relevant training aids

The possible training aids that can be used effectively in the demonstration are listed below, in order of decreasing impact, if they are used as singular aids. Even the less impactive aids can become more useful when combined with other aids.

- The object itself
- A video of the process
- A 3-D computer graphic
- A video projection
- A photograph of the object
- A line diagram of the object
- A process line chart
- A process description handout

The object itself

The object, if sufficiently small and portable, can be brought to the training room, set up in view of the learning group and used in both the descriptive and demonstration phases. In other cases when the object is too large or is immovable, the group can be taken to the object for the actual description and demonstration. In some cases the full session can be held at the location of the object.

A video of the process

A good quality video showing all aspects of the object or operation can be used if the object itself is not available. This video can be commercially produced or cheaply and simply made by the trainer with a home video camera. The essential inclusion is clear repre-sentation of every step or part, preferably, where relevant, from different viewpoints.

A 3-D computer graphic

Excellent graphic software is widely available for computer projection of line drawings or photographs, with 3-D effects and even skeletal breakdowns in which internal features can also be demonstrated. This latter feature can sometimes be superior to seeing the object operating, but with only the external features visible.

A video projection

The training aid that uses a modified overhead projector plus a video camera is described in Chapter 6. Basically it is an aid that can demonstrate the appearance and/or operation of small pieces of equipment with a visual projection on to a screen that is visible to the full group.

A photograph of the object

A photograph is in many cases the simplest, the easiest and most effective form of visual representation of the object when it is not possible to have the object itself available. The aid can be an actual photograph, enlarged to the maximum extent possible, or a transparency that can be projected on a large screen. A series of photographs can show the object from a number of angles, but the approach suffers from lack of movement.

A line diagram of the object

The simplest visual representation of an object is a sketch or line drawing, shown to the learning group usually as a flipchart poster or as an OHP slide.

A process line chart

This is more relevant when a flowing operation is being described, the complete process being listed in a progressive manner, the chart being projected as an OHP slide, entered on a pre-prepared flipchart, entered on a flipchart sheet with information extracted from the learning group, or circulated on paper.

A process description handout

This would be similar to the process line chart, but might be the only way in which the information could be given to the learners – as a stand-alone this would be less than effective. However, as a reinforcing or reminder handout to be issued following an event, it will frequently be an important part of the learning process.

AN AID TO MATCHING AIDS TO METHODS

Figure 2.2 gives a working summary of the principal training aids for the training approaches listed earlier.

TRAINING METHOD	Activities	Chalk boards	Combined projector	Episcope	Flip-charts	Handouts	OHP	35mm slides	Objects	The trainer	IV/Computer	Whiteboard
ACTIVITIES	✓				✓	✓	✓		✓		✓	✓
CASE STUDIES		✓			✓	✓	✓		✓		✓	✓
CBT/IV						✓					✓	
DEMONSTRATIONS			✓		✓				✓	✓	✓	
GROUP DISCUSSIONS		✓			✓	✓	✓			✓		✓
INPUT SESSION/ PRESENTATIONS		✓	✓	✓	✓	✓	✓	✓	✓	✓	✓	✓
1 TO 1 INSTRUCTION			✓		✓	✓	✓	✓	✓	✓	✓	✓
PROJECTS	✓				✓	✓						✓
ROLE PLAYS	✓				✓	✓			✓			✓

Figure 2.2 *Training aids and training methods*

AN AID TO SELECTION

An aid can be constructed to assist in the selection process, matching the range of available aids against a number of criteria. Figure 2.3 demonstrates a matrix that can be modified according to your own equipment and materials, and the range of aids appropriate.

The completed matrix can be included in your training file for the particular event and consequently will act as a permanent (but revisable) record that will remind you of the needs for your event. Completed at an early stage in the planning of the event it acts as a trigger to remind you what you require compared with what you already have.

How many aids to use?

It is difficult to be completely definitive in answering this question as much will depend on the length of the session, its complexity, the nature of the subject and the group involved. However, each trainer or presenter must address the question when planning and designing the session. It may be useful to bear in mind the problems of attention span and the possibility of avoiding these by varying the session with interesting and useful aids. Too many visual aids can annoy some learners, who prefer to concentrate their learning senses on listening intently and weighing up the information they receive. Others (the ones who prefer to use visual senses) will welcome an appropriate number of images which they can look at and digest.

One of the problems for trainers and presenters is that they may not be aware of the learning preferences of their groups or, more commonly, the group consists of a completely heterogeneous collection of learners. In this case provided the subject, etc is consistent with the use of aids it is usually most effective to include them rather than rely on your (possibly imagined) presentation charisma. But do not include too many, otherwise you will defeat their purpose. Perhaps the criterion to follow is to have aids available for the significant learning points in the session – the 'must knows' and some of the 'should knows' of session planning.

The non-availability of sophisticated equipment should be no excuse for not including aids where they are relevant. As we shall see later, very mundane objects can be excellent training aids – for example, a number of A4 sheets of paper can be taped together to form a poster-sized sheet if a commercial flipchart sheet is not available. The taped result may not look professional, but if the alternative is to use nothing when a poster is essential, there really is no choice.

CRITERIA	Chalk-boards	Flip-charts	White-board	OHP	35mm slides	Combined projector	Episcope	Videos	Computer program	Interactive videos	Objects	Handouts	Work books
Equipment available		✓	✓	✓				✓				✓	
Can obtain equipment		✓	✓	✓									
Environment suitable		✓	✓	✓				✓					
Time to prepare etc												✓	

Figure 2.3 *Selection matrix example*

Some complex sessions require the use of a number of training aids, or the trainer has decided that they would be useful. Different aids used in a session can make it more interesting and educative – provided their use does not interrupt the session's flow. I have attended a session at which the trainer had two flipcharts – one on each side of the room; a whiteboard mounted behind him; an OHP with a large screen projector facility; a video, video player and monitor; and a computer to show about 30 seconds of a program. The session was a disaster. His perpetual movement from chart to chart to whiteboard to chart, and so on, fazed the participants. To make matters worse, it soon became obvious that he had not prepared as thoroughly as he might have done (or there were too many aids to remember) as hesitancy and confusion over which aid to use started to creep in. The final catastrophe of a mounting number of these was his intention to play part of a video, without having found the relevant section beforehand. In the end the trainer decided publicly not to use the video, the relevant part never having been found.

This account is a true anecdote, and may be thought an extreme case, but things can go wrong even with a smaller number of pieces of equipment to stage manage on your own. If you are not sure whether or not you can cope with what you want to use, have a strictly controlled rehearsal – if anything goes wrong in this you can be certain that it will in the live event, too (and according to a certain person's law other things will also go wrong!).

Cost

Costs of purchase, hire and/or production can reduce the number of training aid options you have. Some of the aspects that may have to be considered include the following.

- Should/can a large capital investment be made to purchase the relevant equipment, software (if appropriate), and perhaps the training necessary in the use of these? Often this initial expense appears too large to justify, but in many cases this disappears in the long term if the materials can be used over and over again
- Should equipment and other materials be hired rather than purchased? Often hire charges are quite high, and if there is going to be repeated hire, purchase often becomes a less expensive option. If, however, the event is to be a one-off, then it would be non-cost effective to purchase, and hiring is obviously the most favoured option.

- If some equipment that you want to hire for a single event is very complex you may be best advised, in spite of the additional expense, to also contract a technical expert to use the equipment for you, rather than take the risk of operating it yourself or, with additional expense, be trained to operate it. Would this latter course be appropriate if the event and use of equipment was unique?

- If you are considering prepared flipcharts or OHP transparencies, how important is it going to be that they appear professional? Remember that you are insulting a learning group by showing them scrappy, dirty, ill-prepared visual aids. Have you a backup organization with an expert in designing and preparing visual aids? If you have, use them. Otherwise, if you have the skill (and the time) you may wish to prepare them yourself. There are organizations that specialize in producing customized aids, but if you have a substantial amount of material expense can mount quickly.

- Where is the session or presentation being held? Will you have to take all your equipment and aids with you or will the equipment at least be available on site? *Check on its availability before you set off for the event!* How far is it from the car park to the location? If there is no help available, a hundred yards is a long way if you have to carry all your own equipment, visual aids, videos, handouts, session briefs, etc! Will your own vehicle be large enough to carry everything you need? Or will you have to hire a more suitable vehicle?

Many of the foregoing questions require you to do a substantial amount of planning at the time you are designing your session or presentation. Do it then and not later – later frequently becomes too late and the resolution of a huge problem may incur large costs that could have been prevented. These comments are certainly relevant for presenters mounting an event within their own organization, but are even more relevant for external providers coming into an organization to provide a service.

Linked with the cost of aids, think about the possibility of:

- borrowing existing material from individuals or organizations that you know have presented similar events
- temporarily modifying existing material, if this is possible, for a one-off event, or making a more permanent modification if the original is no longer used and a series of new events are to take place

■ making in-house videos instead of contracting their making to specialist producers, even if the 'amateur' result is not as polished as the professional one would be – is a Rolls-Royce needed for a Mini purpose?!

3

—

Chalkboards; Flipcharts; Whiteboards – Common Techniques

The training aids listed in Chapter 2 included both visual and audio aids, the former identifying what are considered the 'traditional' visual aids. Three of these – the chalkboard, the flipchart and the whiteboard – have very similar characteristics.

THE CHALKBOARD

The *chalkboard* is the generic name for the traditional, once ubiquitous blackboard, so called because it was black, but nowadays as likely to be green. It is a large rectangle of wood, coated with a surface which can be written on with chalk, usually white, but also in a range of colours. One useful facility is that the chalk marking can be erased easily with a cloth or special blackboard eraser – this can, however, work as much against its use as for it, as the chalk is easily smudged or erased by mistake. The board is either mounted on a large wooden or metal three-legged easel, which can be set at different heights to suit the user or the learning group, or mounted permanently on a wall.

Little use is made of the chalkboard in training events nowadays, although at one time it was in very common use – certainly up to 12 to 15 years ago in my experience – and it can still be seen, most usually in school classrooms or on café walls. Apart from being messy it suffered from a limited portability because of its size and weight, and it has been mainly superseded by its successors – the flipchart, the whiteboard and the OHP.

THE FLIPCHART

The *flipchart* is a more flexible and portable version of the chalkboard, having a smaller easel to which is usually attached a metal sheet, normally glossy, white coated and frequently magnetic. You can write on this sheet with special, erasable marker pens, or letters and graphics fitted with small magnets can be affixed, but usually it serves as the base support for the flipchart itself, a pad of paper of A1 size (585 mm × 810 mm). The pad's sheets having been used can be 'flipped' over the top of the easel and out of the way – hence the name 'flipchart'. The flipchart has evolved over the past 20 years or so from packs of sheets of fairly thin, light brown paper referred to as newsprint, to well-produced, high quality pads of paper, usually white, but also obtainable in various colours, including black, and with reusable surfaces.

THE WHITEBOARD

A *whiteboard* is a white, metal board, usually rectangular in shape and ranging in size from A4 to huge, covering large areas of a wall. The metal sheet is commonly coated with a vitreous enamel surface that can be written on with special marker pens. Most whiteboards use a dry-wipe surface enabling the markings to be erased easily with a dry cloth or a felt pad – this dry-wipe surface has almost completely replaced the earlier versions that needed a wet cloth or special cleaner to erase the markings. It is essential to use the correct marker pens otherwise the entries can only be erased with a special cleaner. It is also wise not to leave written entries on the board for too long, as with the dry cloth a smear or image can be left behind, particularly with well-used boards.

Many whiteboards are made of magnetic material so that letters or objects fitted with small magnets can be affixed temporarily and moved about as desired. Small magnets or sheets and strips of magnetic rubber can be bought. Images can then be fixed to these magnets which can be placed on the magnetized whiteboard and left or moved around. A typical use is in football tactics training. The whiteboard, marked as appropriate, represents the playing area and figure symbols can be moved to different positions to demonstrate tactics. Figure 3.1 shows a simple example of this.

The surface is usually glossy, but can be matt and can be used as a projector screen. The normal board colour is white, but coloured 'white' boards can be obtained.

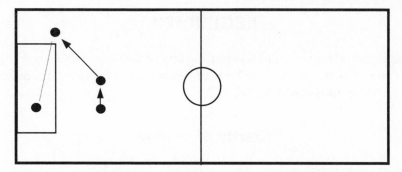

Figure 3.1 *A use for a magnetic whiteboard*

The smaller whiteboards, up to about A1 size, can usually be mounted on easels, or are even integral parts of an easel, but a lighter, smaller and more portable easel than the one used for the chalkboard. Small whiteboards, of say A4 size, can be used as notebooks or memo pads in one-to-one or very small group situations – I have used one such when facilitating a group of six senior managers seated around a table.

Larger whiteboards are less portable and are usually fixed to the wall of the training room, either as a permanent fixture or on display rails, thus being capable of being moved to different positions for easier group view or moved out of direct sight. These are frequently found nowadays in custom-built training rooms rather than rooms that have been pressed into service for training purposes.

More recent developments of the whiteboard include multiboard units. These can be standard size boards but with double-sided writing boards and flipchart holders, capable of rotation of the board. Or they can be large assemblies containing three or more screens that can be electrically rotated horizontally on a continuous belt, so that successive screens can be used and referred back to when needed. These latter complex and expensive units or even single boards can also be fitted with an electronic device that can provide, at the touch of a switch, multiple paper copies at A4 size of what has been written on the board/screen in a matter of seconds. A far cry from the dusty blackboard!

COMMON TECHNIQUES

The three aids described above and the materials associated with them require the use of the written word or graphic image, and many of the techniques used are common to all. These common techniques are described here, modifications between the aids being explained in the relevant part of this chapter.

LEGIBILITY

The principal requirement when using any of the three aids is legibility, in order that the entries can be read easily by the learners. A number of factors contribute to legibility.

Clarity of writing

The marker pens used for group visibility are thick pointed, so as to produce distinctive lettering. The size of the lettering is greater than that to which most people are accustomed and consequently, if you have not used the pens and aids previously, some practice is recommended. You should aim to write larger than you think you need to do, as we are more accustomed to writing on A4 or smaller paper. The lettering should usually be about 2–3 inches in height, although this can vary depending on the size of the group and their proximity to the aid. A rule of thumb is a height of 2 inches (50 mm) when the group is about 20 feet (6 metres) away, increasing in size by about half an inch (13 mm) for every additional 10 feet (3 metres).

The most important criterion for this lettering or image is that it should be easily readable by all the group, which in practice means by the person furthest away from the aid. When you are pre-preparing a flipchart poster or know that you will have to write on the flipchart/whiteboard during a session, experiment before the event by trying out different sizes, colours, etc and viewing the aid from that point in the room where the furthest learner will be placed.

Quality of writing

The obvious necessity to ensure legibility is that the writing, in addition to the factors mentioned above, must be of good quality. If words are being written, the letters must be well formed and identifiable – some people have particular ways of writing certain letters or abbreviations that may not be clear to others. Examine your writing for idiosyncrasies and ensure that you regularize them if you have to write in public. The simpler the form of the letters the better – usually a block type of font with no serifs (the extensions to letters) except perhaps for an upper case 'I' rather than 'I' which might be misinterpreted as the figure 1. Always remember that other people have to read your writing, usually from a distance and not necessarily under the best lighting conditions.

Block printing is usually preferable to script, because it is not only clearer but there is less likelihood that carelessness will creep in.

However, if your script is very well formed and clear (check it out from the back of the group), then use this, particularly when using the aid as a recording pad for comments from the group during a session.

There is frequently a disagreement over whether UPPER or lower case should be used and whether an aid should be written in one or the other completely. The choice will often depend on the preference and ease of writing of an individual trainer, and there does not seem to be any strong argument for either. One compromise, reflected from A4 report writing, is to write the headline and headings in upper case, and the subhead entries in lower case, starting usually with an upper case letter. There is some evidence that lower case with upper case first letters is more readable and less boring to look at than entries all in upper case. Try the different approaches out yourself and decide with which you are most comfortable and which are sufficiently legible for the learning group.

Figures 3.2, 3.3 and 3.4 demonstrate the same poster in three different styles – which do you prefer and which might your learners prefer?

VISUAL AIDS

LEGIBILITY

CLARITY OF WRITING

QUALITY OF WRITING

GRAPHICS

USE OF COLOUR

USE OF BOXES

UNDERLINING

AIM FOR CLARITY AND IMPACT

Figure 3.2 *Poster in upper case only*

Visual aids

Legibility

Clarity of writing

Quality of writing

Graphics

Use of colour

Use of boxes

Underlining

Aim for clarity and impact

Figure 3.3 *Poster in lower case only, with upper case first letter*

VISUAL AIDS

LEGIBILITY

Clarity of writing

Quality of writing

Graphics

Use of colour

Use of boxes

Underlining

AIM FOR CLARITY AND IMPACT

Figure 3.4 *Poster in upper case headings and impact line, remainder in lower case with upper case first letter*

LAYOUT AND BREVITY

The way in which you lay out your chalkboard/flipchart/whiteboard poster can have considerable impact on its clarity and legibility, as well as giving it a pleasant appearance. The fewer the number of lines (well placed on the poster) the more appealing and impactive – aim wherever possible for no more than eight to ten lines. The number of words on each line should be similarly constrained – no more than six or seven words; fewer than this is even better. If the poster becomes too crowded it will start to lose any impact you intended.

The exception to these 'rules' is when you are writing on the aid during a session, perhaps when taking views or feedback from the group and recording these comments. You can in this situation afford to enter more on a poster, but still try to obey the rules of clarity and quality of writing. Try to avoid the bottom part of the poster as this may be obscured from the sight of those at the rear of the group.

Figures 3.2, 3.3 and 3.4 demonstrate posters or whiteboard entries with nine lines and a maximum, on one line, of five words. Figure 3.5 demonstrates the same poster modified to include more material with resulting reduced clarity. Notice that the size of letters has had to be reduced to enable all the material to be included.

LEGIBILITY

- Writing must be clear so that it can be read easily by all the members of the group
- The quality of writing will determine its legibility, particularly from the rear of the group
- Graphics can be more easily read than writing and learners may appreciate pictures more than words
- Use of colour — this will make the poster more pleasant in appearance and can be used to link ideas or make parts stand out
- Use boxes around words or phrases to make the boxed entry stand out as important from the remainder of the writing
- Underlining will make a word or phrase stand out from those not underlined
- Aim for clarity and impact by using the various techniques

Figure 3.5 *An example of a 'cluttered' poster*

> **Remember that a training aid is meant to support the speaker, not replace the spoken word, so consequently keep your poster messages short, sharp and simple.**

Leave out non-essential words and consider using abbreviations – but ensure that these are universally recognized, not ones that you have invented.

Identification

Wherever possible, include at the top of the poster (whether a pre-prepared one or one produced during the session) a short heading that identifies the topic of the poster and also helps the members of the learning group focus their attention on the topic. If sheets are torn from a flipchart, rather than flipped over, but are wanted at a later stage, the heading can help you to pick out the required sheet.

At times it is desirable to retain a sheet during an event or for action afterwards, and if there is more than one sheet in such a series numbers should be added to remind you of the order later, when the event might not be too clear in your mind.

Both these identification tips will help you to avoid puzzling over the sheets at a later stage when you have to refer to them and take action.

Colour

There is no regulation that states that your chalkboard entry should be written with white chalk or the flipchart and whiteboard markings with black markers only. There is colour in life and we are used to seeing this – compare the preference of television viewers between monochrome and colour television. Use colour freely on your posters or whiteboard entry to:

- Link connected ideas
- Emphasize certain words or phrases
- Pick out the more important entries
- Start a word with a different colour from the rest of the word or phrase to clarify the start of that part

Although a book printed in monochrome cannot show colours, as in real life you can mimic colours by varying shades of grey or depth of shading – this is certainly possible on a poster.

Be careful in your choice of colours and do not be tempted to use too many – 'a coat of many colours' on a training aid poster may defeat the objective. Concentrate on two or three strong colours – blue, red, green, violet; headings might be in red; subheads in green; and the remainder in blue or violet. Avoid pale colours – yellow and pinks – as they do not show up well, particularly in poorer lighting conditions, even more so if the marker itself is starting to fade.

Also be careful about using colours on your posters and referring to items as 'the line in blue' – some people have colour deficiencies and that statement may mean nothing to them

As with the size of lettering, when you have experimented with colours or shading, go to the rear of the room and assess the poster's legibility.

OTHER FORMS OF IMPACT

Bullets

There is again some disagreement about whether there is a place for bullets on a poster or whiteboard/chalkboard aid. Those who are against it say that it can confuse, adds images the result of which can be achieved by other impactive means, and complicates line and word positioning – should a short bulleted line be centred, or left aligned?

If you use bullets to emphasize lines or words, and there can be no doubt that they draw attention to these, keep the bullet simple. It is tempting to use such symbols as ●, ■, □, ◎, ✳, ✶, ◆, ⌘ or ☉, but their use can be addictive and their overuse annoying. Stick to one or two – I am usually constrained by my publishers to ■ and ●. Figures 3.6 and 3.7 demonstrate bulleted lists centred and left aligned – which do you prefer?

Underlining

Another method of attempting <u>to add impact to words or phrases in your poster is to underline them</u>, <u>with either single or double</u> underlining. As with any other effect used for emphasis, be careful not to overdo it – if everything is underlined, then nothing stands out, just as if nothing had been underlined.

VISUAL AIDS

- **LEGIBILITY**
- Clarity of writing
- Quality of writing
- Graphics
- Use of colour
- Use of boxes
- Underlining

■ **AIM FOR CLARITY AND IMPACT**

Figure 3.6 *Centred bulleted poster*

VISUAL AIDS

LEGIBILITY

- Clarity of writing
- Quality of writing
- Graphics
- Use of colour
- Use of boxes
- Underlining

■ **AIM FOR CLARITY AND IMPACT**

Figure 3.7 *Left-aligned bulleted poster with heading and footing centred*

Boxes

Boxes are among the most effective methods of isolating parts of a poster for emphasis. They can be either:

```
┌─────────────────────────────────────────┐
│  Simply boxed with single lines, thin     │
└─────────────────────────────────────────┘
```

or

```
┏━━━━━━━━━━━━━━━━━━━━━━━━━━━━━━━━━━━━━━━━━━┓
┃  Boxed with single lines, thick           ┃
┗━━━━━━━━━━━━━━━━━━━━━━━━━━━━━━━━━━━━━━━━━━┛
```

or

```
╔═════════════════════════════════════════╗
║  Boxed with double lines                  ║
╚═════════════════════════════════════════╝
```

Whichever form of box you use, there are two principal caveats:

1. Write the word or phrase first then enclose it with a box, rather than the other way round, or you may find you have made the box too small.
2. As with colours, underlines, etc, use boxes in a controlled way, otherwise the impact may be lost.

SPECIFIC TECHNIQUES

CHALKBOARDS AND FLIPCHARTS

The techniques for using both chalkboards and flipcharts are so similar that they will be covered together, the principal differences being the ease of smudging and erasing, and the difficult aspects of permanency for the chalkboard. Both demand the careful use of writing techniques described previously, and the following guidance should be read with the obvious differences in mind. Reference will be made mainly to the flipchart; relating any minor differences from the chalkboard will be quite simple and straightforward.

Uses

The principal uses for the flipchart in training and development include those shown in Figure 3.8.

```
■  POSTER SHOWING AIMS AND OBJECTIVES

■  PROVIDING DISCUSSIONS SUBJECT FOCUS

■  SUPPORTING TRAINER'S PRESENTATION

■  COLLECTING VIEWS FROM LEARNING GROUP
```

Figure 3.8 *Uses of chalkboards and flipcharts in training and development*

Pre-prepared poster

In a course or workshop with a duration of more than a day, the sheer variety of subjects raised for discussion (some of which may vary from the specific aims and objectives of the event) may mean that some may be lost sight of. If they are entered on a flipchart or chalkboard, and displayed in a prominent position for the duration of the event, they are a constant reminder to you and the learners of the objectives towards which they should be moving.

A modification of this is the use of a flipchart by the trainer to record the learners' objectives.

One useful and interesting method of group introductions is to ask each learner to enter comments on certain questions on a part-prepared flipchart. The completed charts are then displayed around the walls of the training room as reminders of where the learners wish to go, etc. Figure 3.9 reproduces an example of such a part-prepared chart.

Another technique frequently used at the start of a training event is to seek from the learners their expectations of and concerns about the event. These views are recorded on a pre-prepared, outline chart on a flipchart sheet.

Again, when the learners have completed this chart, it is displayed in the training room for reference at the end of the event.

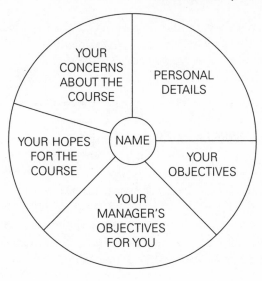

Figure 3.9   *A part-prepared chart for learner introductions*

Figure 3.10 suggests the form of one of these charts, commonly referred to as T-charts.

EXPECTATIONS AND CONCERNS T-CHART

Expectations/Hopes	Concerns/Worries

Figure 3.10   *Expectations/Concerns T-Chart*

Providing a focus

In a similar way to displaying the course objectives, more limited aims can be displayed as a reminder to all involved and also, when concentration is needed, as a physical focus. For example, when a structured discussion is being held, the subject of the discussion can be displayed in front of the group – basically this will remind the participants what they should be discussing, but by the simple act of looking at the words mental images can form with subsequent opinions emerging.

Supporting the trainer's presentation

This, of course, is the one traditional purpose of the visual aid, and a series of these pre-prepared sheets act as supports during the presentation. Say the session consists of six key areas – this may result in six flipchart sheets, each concentrating on one key area and containing the subheadings of that area. As the session or presentation proceeds the aids are referred to, using the variety of additive or disclosure methods that will be described later. In this way, they thus support and reinforce your verbal presentation, but do not replace it.

Collecting views from the learning group

This is the other traditional use for the flipchart. You might ask for the views, opinions, or knowledge of the full learning group on a particular subject as part of the session – these responses are then written on a flipchart sheet for discussion and/or subsequent posting on the wall of the training room. Or, if the full group is divided into smaller sub-groups, each with a task to perform and report back on, they may write on flipcharts displayed at the front of the group during their presentation of their findings. A third use, combining the first two, would be for you to complete a flipchart while taking the verbal report backs from the sub-groups. A modification of this third approach would be to have a pre-prepared chart, covered in a material on which task results could be written, and erased when no longer required. In the *Lego Mast* activity, for example, the number of Lego bricks, time used and height of mast achieved are recorded on such a sheet showing the profit or loss achievements of each group.

Even if the reported comments are not to be retained, learning is almost always supported if verbal comments are also summarized in writing.

So the flipchart is not just the simple sheet of paper that it appears to be at first acquaintance. Used appropriately it can be a very effective form of training and learning aid.

A second flipchart

A useful tip if you have a number of pre-prepared flipcharts, but also intend to take feedback from the group and use the flipchart as the recording or scribbling pad, is to have two flipcharts on separate stands. Keep one for your prepared posters and the other for completion during the session. In this way you won't lose your place in your order of posters.

ADVANTAGES

The flipchart has many advantages compared with other training aids. In summary these are:

- Simple to use
- Highly portable
- No power required
- Relatively cheap
- Versatile
- Sheet 'flipping'
- Ease of use
- Ease of writing

Simple to use

If you can write or draw, you can use it, although effective use requires practice.

Highly portable

The flipchart paper can be rolled to take up minimal space, and the easel or stand can be folded and sometimes reduced in size with sliding legs.

No power source required

Consequently there is no interruption due to power cuts or electrical component failure.

Relatively cheap

Once the easel or other paper support is purchased (typically about £60–£80 in the UK in 1998) all that is required are pads of flipchart paper (typically about £2–£3 a pad) and long-lasting (provided the caps are replaced when the pen is not in use!) marker pens at about £5 per set of 12 different colours.

Versatile

Some of the many uses have been described above, but the versatility extends to the paper and the use of 'stands'. Although the paper used is normally purchased in flipchart pads, any large sheet of paper can be used, smaller than the easel or trimmed to size if necessary. Standard flipchart paper can be used, but it is also possible to obtain pads with ready-made perforations near the top of the sheet to ease removal, and coated paper from which entries (made with special pens) can be erased after use.

Most flipchart stands are equipped at the top with metal posts and the pads are slipped on to these by means of holes cut in the pads; or a large clip forms the top of the stand into or by which the pad can be clipped in place. But a stand is not essential. Using a product such as Blutack sheets of paper can be fixed temporarily to doors, windows, cabinet doors and even curtains, either before use or for posting purposes.

Sheet 'flipping'

Once a sheet has been used it can be flipped over the top of the stand to reveal the next sheet and hide the entries made on the used sheet. Or it can be torn off the pad and retained in a pile, posted on the training room wall, or simply wasted.

Ease of use

Although posters are improved with the types of writing techniques previously described, these techniques are not essential, particularly if unskilled learners are preparing flipcharts as report-back memo pads.

Ease of writing

Even with the constraints already mentioned, learners can write on flipcharts quite easily and legibly (although they get better with practice) and most people find them easier to write on than whiteboards and overhead projector slides.

DISADVANTAGES

In the same way that flipcharts have advantages and benefits as visual aids, so they also have some disadvantages, although most have considerably less impact than the advantages. The major disadvantages are summarized below.

- Writer turning away from the group
- Restricted sheet size
- Writing difficulties
- Unprofessional looking
- Easily damaged
- Special effects not as easy

Writer turning away from group

Writing on a flipchart during a session demands the use of special techniques to avoid or minimize the effects of turning away from the group while writing. This aspect of flipchart use will be described later in this chapter.

Restricted sheet size

Because an A1 flipchart sheet is 585 x 810 mm, thicker pens than for ordinary writing need to be used and the lettering has to be larger than on, say, an A4 sheet of paper. Consequently the writer might feel restricted, although the techniques of using minimal words should avoid most of this problem.

Writing difficulties

It was mentioned in the advantages that almost anyone who can write can do so on a flipchart. However, there is considerable difference between writing with an ordinary pen on an A4 sheet in a normal size, and doing so on an A1 sheet with thick pens and large lettering. However, practice improves this skill for almost every learner.

Unprofessional appearance

Because the medium is *only* a sheet of paper it can often be taken for granted, and insufficient care taken in producing it either in pre-preparation or during a session. Consequently the sheet takes on a scribbled, unprofessional appearance that not only discredits you but can inhibit learning. Learners may not actively appreciate a flipchart with a professional appearance, but the reverse certainly applies.

Easily damaged

Because the flipchart is a paper product considerable care must be taken to ensure that it is not damaged in transit or storage. It is easy for sheets to be torn, or become dirty or dog-eared unless care is taken. Preventative measures include carrying and storing the sheets in roll-containers or, particularly if the chart is to be used frequently, covering them with a transparent protective film. Although not a physical problem, as with any other permanent training aid, care must be taken that the content is kept up to date with both organizational practice and the current training brief.

Special effects not easy

Although it is relatively easy to produce special effects on a flipchart (such as different forms of graphic image and the technique of disclosure) these are not as easy to do as with some other aids, particularly the OHP. However, with care and flexibility it is possible to transform a flipchart into something considerably more than just a sheet of paper on which are written a number of words. This includes using the many impact-making forms of lettering, picture inclusion, disclosure cards and also additive features, such as pointers, large asterisks and masks that can be temporarily fixed to the sheet.

FLIPCHART TECHNIQUES

Techniques for using flipcharts can be summarized as:

- FLIPCHART WRITING
- CONTENT
- USING THE SHEETS THEMSELVES
- PRE-PREPARATION TECHNIQUES

Writing on the flipchart

A number of guidelines can be given in addition to those described in the preceding section of common techniques for the chalkboard, flipchart and whiteboard.

Talking to the flipchart

Using the flipchart while writing requires a degree of skill and technique, although the users' preferences and abilities may decide which of the two principal techniques is more suitable.

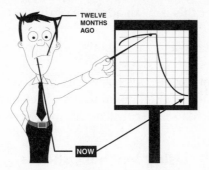

The common guideline is that you should not talk *at* the flipchart while you are writing on it, usually when you have your back to the group. This is the major disadvantage in using the flipchart – it is only too easy to turn away from the group, something that should be avoided as much as possible, although it may be necessary on occasion.

One frequently used approach is to stand at the side of the flipchart as you are writing so you are not completely turned away from the group. The problem with this approach, not confined to inexperienced writers only, is that as you write and stretch across to the other side of the chart your lines start to drift downwards towards the bottom of the chart. This gives an untidy, unprofessional appearance that can distract from the learning. Also, depending on your height, you may have to stretch in an ungainly manner across the board as you write.

One alternative that minimizes the downsloping is to face the chart squarely while writing. Unfortunately this means that your back is towards the group while you are writing.

So, unless you are experienced and skilled in writing from the side and are tall enough to reach easily across the chart, facing the chart to write is your best option. But while you are facing away from the group:

- do not talk, as your words may be lost in the flipchart
- write as quickly and as little as possible on each occasion, unless you have to scribe verbatim.

Some people have suggested talking more loudly than usual if you are facing the chart – in my experience this is rarely successful. Accept that your back is to the group, and follow the suggestions above.

The content

Here is a summary of the guidelines regarding the content of what you write, whether this is in an additive or disclosure form.

- KISS – particularly if you might otherwise have to use a lot of words on a lot of lines.
- Limit one sheet to one subject, and always have a heading.
- Get into the habit of thinking in terms of key words and short key phrases rather than well-constructed, long sentences.

Using flipchart sheets

Guidelines for using flipchart sheets include the following.

- When finished with a sheet always either:
  - flip the sheet over the top of the stand
  - tear off the sheet and post for subsequent reference
  - tear off and destroy.
- When you know sheets will have to be torn off the pad, unless the pad already has perforations, lightly score the sheet a few millimetres from the top.

- Have fine lines drawn lightly across blank sheets on which you will have to write during the session to help your lines stay horizontal.

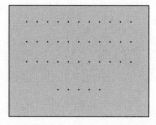

- Have the outlines of pictures lightly drawn on the sheets when these will have to be completed during the session.
- Lightly outline words that you know will have to be added to the sheets during the session.

The light pencil marks mentioned above will be seen by you only; the group will be too far away to see them.

Pre-preparation

Whenever possible and relevant you will be preparing your session flipcharts in advance, usually when you are planning the session and writing the session brief. Guidelines for using the flipchart at this stage are as follows.

- Those suggested for action during the session, but in this case, to help you make your chart entries clearer, neater and more professional looking, draw faint pencil lines across the chart where you will be writing. These can be erased before the session, but this may not be necessary as if they are faint they will not be seen in any case by the group.
- Enter at this stage the lines, outlines and cribs mentioned above, again in faint pencil so they will not eventually be seen.
- Draw your proposed graphic images or pictures on the charts.
- Produce your 'disclosure technique' masks.

The last item above requires some comment.

Producing images and pictures

If you are an excellent artist or cartoonist you should use your talents to the maximum extent, making your flipcharts as graphic as possible, whether in support of the words or as stand-alone images. Most of us, however, are not sufficiently talented to produce attractive and recognizable images – apart from matchstick people, and sometimes not even these! There are a number of possibilities. One is to find a picture, drawing or photograph that already exists and use this to illustrate your chart. The principal problem, even discounting the difficulty of finding what you want, is that once fixed to a flipchart it is too small to be useful or seen easily from a distance. This means that in some way you are going to have to draw!

Usually the image you require does exist in some form or other and it is then necessary to use a projection technique to transfer the image on to your flipchart. The process is as follows:

1. Fix the flipchart sheet to a wall with something like Blutack.
2. Project the image of the picture or drawing on to the flipchart to the required size and in the required position.
3. Draw round the outline of the projected image and add other lines and markings that are essential to the finished image.
4. Add whatever colour is necessary.

This process sounds simple, and is, apart sometimes from the projection of the image, for which you will need special equipment. If the original image is a drawing, diagram or photograph, that is, a solid object, you will need an episcope. This is a projection instrument for such objects that, by producing an illuminated reflection of the object, an image is projected on a screen so that you can trace round it.

If the image is on an OHP transparency you simply project the image via the OHP on to the flipchart and complete the tracing.

An alternative method of increasing the size of the original small image is to enlarge it by using a photocopier. This can be by increasingly larger image copying or by copying the enlarged image on to a number of A4 sheets that are then joined together.

THE DISCLOSURE TECHNIQUE

The additive technique refers to writing or drawing on the flipchart during the session. The disclosure method is used when the flipchart is pre-prepared, but so constructed that:

- not all the chart is disclosed at once
- the items on the chart can be disclosed one at a time
- the order of disclosure is flexible.

The flipchart will normally show a list of words or phrases, or perhaps the stages of a process that will be discussed during a session. If the whole chart is displayed while you are speaking about, say, item two, the group will read on and may have reached item six, possibly having missed a lot of what you were saying and also not necessarily understanding the forward stages.

There are two main techniques for dealing with this.

In the first case, if there are only two or three items on the chart, the sheet can be folded (and held by Blutack or paper clips) to hide the items following the first. As each entry is to be discussed it can be disclosed by unfolding the relevant fold. The principal disadvantage invokes 'Murphy', as at inopportune times the folds can come undone.

The second technique is certainly easier to use and is more professional looking. When there are more than two or three entries, or when folding does not appear appropriate, disclosure masks can be made. These are rectangular pieces of paper, or preferably card, cut sufficiently large to cover each entry individually. They can be held to the chart by Blutack or, if they extend to the edges of the chart, by paper clips. When the session reaches the entry to be discussed it is 'disclosed' by the simple expedient of removing the relevant mask.

Advantages

The advantages of this approach are that:

- the group cannot read in advance items that you have not reached
- you are not restricted to disclosing the items in order, as you would be with the folds, and can select the entries according to the way in which you have run that part of the session on this occasion.

Disadvantages

Two disadvantages to the disclosure technique are apparent, 'apparent' because only one is a real disadvantage.

The apparent one is that the entries in the chart are covered by the masks, and unless you can remember what is underneath you may disclose the wrong item. This can be simply remedied by using the ubiquitous faint pencil marking. On the mask write faintly an indication of what is underneath. Again, you will be able to see this crib but the learning group will not.

The real problem when you have a chart with a number of entries covered is that some of the learning group may engage in the silent guessing game of what is hidden, and also, as you disclose some items, they start counting how many are left! Both these might contribute to non-listening, but unfortunately there is nothing you can do to avoid this other than ensure in some other way that they listen actively and take part in the session by question and answer, discussion, etc.

Figure 3.11 shows part of a disclosure flipchart format.

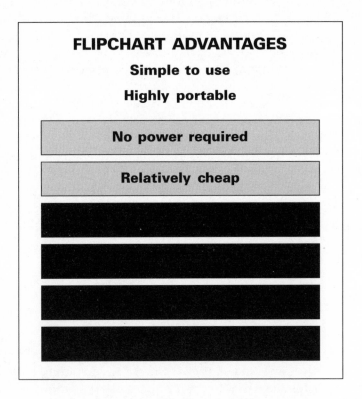

Figure 3.11 *Part of a disclosure flipchart format*

MISCELLANEOUS GUIDELINES

■   Before you start the session ensure that there is sufficient paper on the flipchart pad (the same applies to flipcharts in syndicate rooms), and that you have spare flipcharts readily available.

- Check that all markers are of the correct type, that you have the required colours, and that they all work.
- Ensure that the easel/stand is stable and properly upright.
- When you pre-prepare a number of flipchart sheets leave a blank sheet between each one so that you do not immediately flip to the next chart – you may not be ready for it. This will also ensure that as you write on the first sheet it does not ink-through to the next.

THE WHITEBOARD

The whiteboard, the later development of the chalkboard and the flipchart, is a metal sheet, usually magnetic, usually coated with a glossy surface on which dry marker pens can be used and erased easily. Whiteboards are usually larger than flipcharts and are frequently mounted permanently on the walls of the training room or are semi-portable, mounted on rail hangers. In some ways they are more a development from the chalkboard than the flipchart as they have some restrictive factors not found in the flipchart.

The uses for the whiteboard are very similar to those for the flipchart, but perhaps rather more limited in pre-preparation as the number of 'posters' is restricted with usually single whiteboard boards and an unlimited number of flipchart sheets. However, some of the additional features of the whiteboard make up for the constraints.

The limited flexibility of the whiteboard is increased by the introduction of electronically operated, multiple sheet whiteboards with their electric sheet movement facilities and the A4 copying facility. However, these models are expensive (about £1500 in the UK in 1998) and limited in their portability because of their size and weight.

Advantages

The advantages of whiteboards include many of those described for the flipchart but there are some additional ones:

- Simple to use
- Entries can be erased and re-entered very easily
- No power required
- Can use magnetic holders
- Versatile
- Cleaner than chalkboard
- Ease of use

- *Simple to use* – no special skills other than those of writing are required.
- *Entries can be erased and re-entered very easily* – the special dry marker pens are very flexible.
- *No power required* – except in the case of the multisheet, electric and electronic whiteboards.
- *Magnetic holders* – these can be used to attach and move signs, graphics, arrows, etc easily.
- *Versatile* – a wide range of the writing and graphic techniques described earlier can be used on the board, in addition to using magnetic holders.
- *Clean* – cleaner than chalkboard as the erased pen marks leave no dust, although they do discolour the cloth or eraser.
- *Ease of use* – apart from practice in the rather more difficult skill of writing on a glossy, slippery surface, no particular skills are required.

Disadvantages

- Facing away from group
- Less easy to use as permanent poster
- Special markers needed
- Writing difficulties
- Unprofessional looking
- Easily erased
- Special effects not easy
- Power cut problems with electronic versions

- As with the flipchart there is the *need to face away from group* when writing, more so when the whiteboard is fixed to the wall at the head of the training room. With fixed boards there may not be room to stand to one side and write.
- *Less easy to use as a permanent poster* because of the likely limited number of whiteboards available and the inability to retain the whiteboard entries after use.
- *Special markers needed* – although these in themselves are not problems, they can be if during a session they run dry and replacements are not immediately available. It may be related to the 'Murphy' effect, but dry marker pens seem to run out faster than any other kind of pen!
- *Writing difficulties* – three aspects of this may cause some problems:
  1. the requirement to stand and write, something of which most people have no experience
  2. writing much larger than that to which most people are accustomed
  3. writing on a glossy, slippery surface.
- *Unprofessional looking* – unless considerable care is taken the board can be covered with untidy writing and drawing, as it is easy to look on a whiteboard, with its erasure facility, as a memo or scribbling pad. Care is particularly important when you are taking feedback from the group and writing down their comments.

  One of the most commonly encountered difficulties when writing on the whiteboard arises because of the size of the board. The majority of boards are large (from about 3 metres by 1.5 metres, the longer side being horizontal), and because of this and the space available, newcomers to the medium tend to spread across the board. The result is frequently a messy board with words and drawings straggling across the whole surface and looking very unprofessional.

  You will find it easier to regulate your use of the whiteboard and produce attractive, readable and controlled results if you look on the large whiteboard as a collection of A1-size flipcharts. When you are entering material on the board, restrict yourself to one, approximately A1-size area of the board. You will find that you have to regulate your thoughts and writing to stay within this area, and your writing and layout will be much improved.
- *Easily erased* – a sleeve or hand can easily brush against the board and smudge or erase the markings. Conversely, if the markings are left on the whiteboard too long (eg several days), particularly if the whiteboard surface is old and has been used a lot, it may be difficult to erase them completely, a smudge or coloured shadow

being left behind which will probably need a special whiteboard cleaner. Short-term use, however, should not cause these problems.

■ *Special effects not easy* – the whiteboard is designed for (and constrained by) writing and drawing and, in most modern cases, magnets. Unless the latter are used the disclosure method is not as simple as in the case of the flipchart and, even with the electronic whiteboard, 'flipped sheets' are restricted to the number of sheet panels contained in the whiteboard.

■ *Power cut problems with electronic versions* – obviously if there is no power the additional facilities of the multisheet whiteboard and the A4 copy-producing capability are no longer available, the whiteboard being reduced to a single sheet board. If a sudden power cut occurred while sheets were being moved and the position was between sheets, even this facility would not be available. Fortunately, cuts of this nature are not common, albeit not unknown.

Flipcharts, whiteboards and, to a much lesser extent, chalkboards, are so common in the training world and so easy to use in a flexible manner that many trainers and presenters rarely use, and see little need for, any other training aid, apart from the OHP that is described in the next section. This is not intended to suggest that trainers *should* restrict themselves to these simpler aids, avoiding other more complex, but extremely useful aids. The criterion must be to use the aids that are most appropriate to the particular situation.

4

Overhead Projectors – 1

Close behind the flipchart and whiteboard in popularity and availability is the overhead projector, universally abbreviated to OHP. It projects images, usually on acetate squares or other transparent film, on to a screen. As shown in Figure 4.1 it consists of a box, A, that contains a light source, projecting light upwards through a semi-opaque glass screen known as a Fresnel Lens, B, the light concentrating on the OHP head, C. In the movable head are a further lens and a reflecting mirror, D. The image on the transparency slide that is placed on the Fresnel Lens is projected on to a screen, usually 5 feet (about 1.5 metres) square and some 4 metres or so away from the OHP. Fitted on the light box is an on/off switch; a switch or lever to reduce refraction discolouring; and (on some models) a switch to move between the main projection bulb and a spare in case the original one burns out. The image is focused by a small wheel fitted to the head that can move up and down the headpost, E.

There is a wide range of OHPs, the differences being the quality of materials used; the features fitted; the interchangeability of the focusing

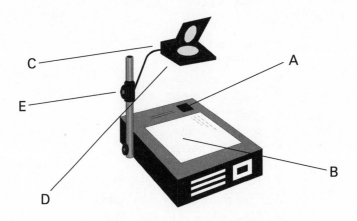

Figure 4.1 *The standard OHP*

lens for enlarged or reduced projected images; silent-running fans or other means of heat dispersion; the availability of projector bulb switching; and the quality of the bulb itself. Some OHPs are fitted to be linked with computers and yet others to large projection equipment. As a result the cost of an OHP can range from (in the UK in early 1998) about £150 to several thousand pounds (one recently advertised with an integrated computer, LCD and OHP, built-in stereo speakers, optical phaser technology and automatic picture elevation level control, etc weighed in at £8,995).

Two principal varieties exist: the standard model described above and a more portable model. In the portable model the base box is considerably reduced in depth, consisting principally of a Fresnel Lens/reflector only. The light is mounted in the head, and consequently the OHP is much lighter in weight and less bulky overall.

The OHP is one of the most flexible training aids generally available and can be very useful to learning because of the range of methods used to project the trainer's approach and the participants' learning.

The projected images can be written and drawn on:

- Acetate squares that can be framed if required
- Other transparent films used in the same way
- Continuous rolls of acetate film that can be wound over and past the Fresnel Lens

  and

- Small solid objects can also be placed on the OHP for silhouette projection

ADVANTAGES

- Wide availability
- Portability
- Group visual contact
- Used standing or sitting
- High visual impact
- Scaleable image
- Relatively cheap
- Small object projection
- Portable transparencies
- Easy transparency production
- Flexibility of use

Wide availability

Few training departments will not have at least one OHP and many offices and other parts of organizations either possess one or can readily obtain one for on-the-job training.

The portable versions really *are* portable

'Portable' frequently means that considerable strength is required. Portable OHPs are sufficiently light to be carried reasonable distances without discomfort.

Projected images are clearly visible in daylight

The projected image is so bright that a darkened room is not necessary, as is the case with some other light projection equipment. This ensures that the OHP has maximum ease of use

The trainer is always facing the group

Unlike the flipchart/whiteboard to which the trainer has to turn, reference is made at the OHP to the transparency laid on the lens. The transparency is placed on the lens so that it is facing the direction of the screen and if you sit to one side, facing the group, the transparency can be easily read. This is shown diagramatically in Figure 4.2.

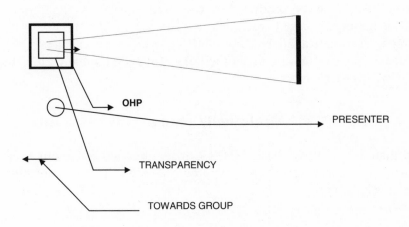

Figure 4.2 *Seating at the OHP for group visibility*

Used standing or sitting

The normal method of use is for the trainer or presenter to sit beside the OHP during the presentation or session, but there is no reason why you should not stand beside it. You may move about a lot during the session, and standing will avoid too much sitting down/standing up. However, the flow of the session can often be helped if you sit down if the OHP is going to be used for a long period, or when it is not being used. When you need to stand up to move over to, eg a flipchart across the room, this movement can help the session by making a break in the continuous process and thus acting as an attention holder.

Whenever you stand up and the OHP is projecting a transparency, ensure that you do not obscure the projected image on the screen. Also resist any temptation to point to the screen, thus turning away from the group, or worse, writing on the screen with the pen you will almost certainly have in your hand!

High visual impact

Because of the large, and particularly the bright image, more notice is likely to be taken of an OHP projection than, say, a flipchart poster. Use this greater impact to ensure that your message is accepted but, because of the impact possibilities, ensure that you control the range of techniques you use.

Image is scaleable

Large images can be produced by the OHP as easily as small ones. This is reasonably easy to control and is limited only by the size of the screen, the space available, the OHP light intensity and lens type. Probably the best to aim for is the largest image possible within the particular environment.

Relatively cheap

As mentioned above, basic OHPs can be obtained for about £150; obviously if more features are required the cost will rise accordingly, but this basic cost is small.

Projects images of small objects

It is not necessary to use only transparent films; small solid objects can be placed on the Fresnel and their shape in silhouette projected on to the screen. This works most effectively if the objects are quite flat and when laid out show clearly what they are, even in silhouette. For example, a key projects well.

Transparencies portable

As they are relatively small pieces of acetate, either squares measuring 250 mm (10 ins) or A4 film measuring 201 mm × 297 mm (8.27 ins × 11.69 ins), transparencies are easily portable. They can be left as they have been produced; mounted on special OHP card frames that leave the correct opening for projection; or inserted into clear acetate sleeves. The last two are recommended particularly if the transparencies are to be retained and used over a period of time.

Ease of transparency production

Transparencies can be manually written, produced with special marker pens – although there are several manufacturers of these, they tend to be generically referred to by the name of one of the earlier makers – Lumocolors made by Staedtler – or professionally produced, photographic transparencies that can be expensive. These methods will be described later, but OHP transparencies are certainly easier to produce than most other aids.

Flexible in use

OHP transparencies can either be pre-prepared or produced during an event, in the same way that we saw with flipchart posters and whiteboard entries. A variety of techniques can also be employed, basically the additive and disclosure, although the latter has more variations than is possible with the flipchart.

DISADVANTAGES

- Needs electricity
- Needs screen
- Annoying illumination
- Obscuring parts
- Noise
- Bulb burnout
- Overcrowding
- Keystoning

Needs electrical power supply

Although these occur rarely nowadays, a power failure or breakdown can happen, and when it does the OHP cannot be operated. This is a timely reminder that the OHP and its transparencies are *aids* to sessions and presentations and should not be used as the session brief. It's a good idea to have one or two activities that do not require power ready to bring into use. These activities could include summary events – 'We've talked about *x* so far; let's try it out in practice.' You will obviously need to have available a number of activities linked to the stages of learning for that particular session; this may not be easy, although you may have some activities prepared in any case, but it is much better than having to say 'Sorry. We can't continue without the power.' The activity will also give you time to consider your next moves!

Needs a screen

An OHP needs a screen or other suitable flat surface on to which the image can be projected. This means that you must ensure that either a screen accompanies the OHP or is available. As a last resort a plain, preferably white wall can be used, as of course can the whiteboard, particularly if the latter's surface is matt.

Light on/off can be annoying

The OHP should rarely be left unused but should be illuminating the screen, with or without a transparency being projected. To avoid this the OHP is usually switched off in between slides, and although this ensures that learners do not continue looking at the slide after it has been used, or the bright, empty square of light does not attract attention to itself rather than to the speaker, the on/off syndrome can also annoy. My own technique is to leave the OHP illuminated if one or two transparencies follow each other quickly, but if there is going to be a gap of a few seconds between them I switch it off.

Head and headpost can obscure

This is probably the most common problem encountered when using an OHP. When you have placed the OHP in what you think is the most favourable position, sit at various points in the room where members of the group will sit to identify problem areas. It might be possible then to move the OHP slightly to rectify these.

Noise

Older and/or cheaper models can be noisy with the heat dispersing fan included in the light box. Later and more expensive OHPs have different, quieter methods of heat dispersal.

Bulb burnout

Projection bulbs do not have an infinite life and 'Murphy' can be invoked again for allowing them to burn out during a presentation. The problem is easily solved on models that have supplementary bulbs to which the projector can be switched. In older and/or cheaper models, if the OHP and its transparencies are essential, the bulb will have to be changed.

Overcrowding

Because it is relatively easy to make entries on an acetate or film transparency there is a temptation – even greater than with a flipchart – to cram on a mass of information: this leads to overcrowding and resultant loss of impact.

Keystoning

This is the effect of producing a distorted image as a result of less than effective setting up of the OHP and screen. This effect and how to avoid it will be described more fully in the following part.

SETTING UP THE OHP AND SCREEN

More than the flipchart or the whiteboard, the OHP and its associated screen require setting up in the training room for optimum effectiveness and use. The following guidance should help in achieving these.

1. Place the OHP on a table so that the head is about 1 metre above the floor. You will need to be prepared to adapt this height in view of problems you may encounter later.
2. Ensure that all lenses and mirrors are clean – you will be surprised by the effect of dust particles or smears, many times enlarged, when projected on to the screen.
3. Set up the screen. The optimum position for this will depend on the size and shape of the training room, and the size and positioning of the group, but in general it is usually best erected across the front left corner of the room, behind and to the right of the trainer or presenter. This will also help to obtain the largest image feasible. Figure 4.3 demonstrates this positioning – the OHP will have to be placed similarly, at an angle facing the screen. This angling in fact helps to make both the OHP screen and the trainer as visible as possible – both desirable attributes from the learning point of view.

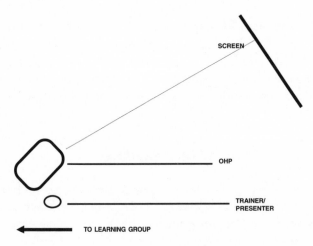

Figure 4.3 *Positioning the OHP and screen*

One of the common problems when setting up an OHP and screen is the effect produced known as 'keystoning'. This is when the projected image has a distorted shape, as shown in Figure 4.4.

TOP

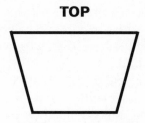

Figure 4.4 *Keystoning*

Keystoning is caused by the light beam from the OHP not being at an angle of 90 degrees with the screen; the more the deviation from this angle, the greater the keystoning effect. This is shown in Figure 4.5, the deviation of the light beam from the 90-degree angle being very obvious.

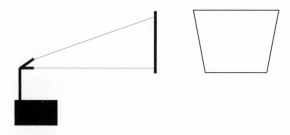

Figure 4.5 *OHP positioning causing keystoning*

Keystoning can be avoided, or minimized, by using the extending arm at the top of the column of most screens. This arm swings out forwards and the screen can be attached to this so that the screen itself is tilted forward. If necessary, the OHP itself can be tilted and with this combination keystoning can be avoided altogether. Care must be taken if the OHP is tilted, however, so that the safety of the OHP and the slides placed upon it are not jeopardized. Figure 4.6 shows this effect.

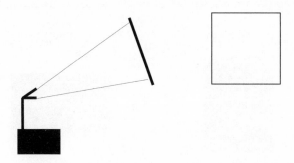

Figure 4.6 *Keystoning avoided by tilting screen*

4.   Ensure that the screen can be seen from all parts of the room. Raising the screen to its maximum height (watch out for keystoning) and moving the screen away from the corner position can help improve visibility.

There are two principal culprits that interrupt the group's view of the screen – the trainer sitting beside the OHP and the headpost of the OHP. Both might be avoided by moving the OHP slightly and the latter by lowering it (again watch out for keystoning). It will obviously be necessary to experiment with different positions of the OHP, screen and trainer to achieve maximum visibility, each move being checked by a colleague trying out various seats. You can yourself check visibility problems caused by the screen and the OHP, but obviously not your own position beside the equipment. In an extreme situation, I have solved this latter problem by using a pile of books on the seat beside the OHP!

5.   The OHP can produce disturbing colour fringes with the screen image, usually blue or red. These can usually be eliminated by using the lever attached to the light box of the OHP. If one is not fitted – as in the case of cheaper, basic OHPs – you may have to readjust the tilt of the OHP and/or screen: back to the problem of keystoning again!

6.   Ensure that the image is in focus by testing with a typical transparency, and again check this from different parts of the room.

7.   Check the projection bulb again and also the spare bulb switching facility, if one is fitted; otherwise, check that you have a spare bulb and know how to fit it.

PREPARING TRANSPARENCIES

Transparency layout

You have two options for the overall layout for your transparency:

PORTRAIT   **LANDSCAPE**

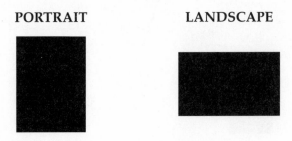

The portrait layout is normally used for slides consisting mainly of words, the landscape frequently for graphics or where large lettering is required.

Writing on the transparency

In many respects preparing a transparency to be used during a session or presentation, using coloured marker pens, is very similar to preparing flipcharts and whiteboards, except that the pens used are much smaller and the size of writing is very similar to the ordinary writing or printing to which people are accustomed. This obviously makes it much easier to prepare an OHP transparency, and even unskilled trainers or presenters can produce something acceptable. With practice a very professional-looking transparency can be produced.

The major principle of the OHP transparency is the same as for any other visual aid: maximum impact using as many of the techniques as are relevant. These include the judicious use of colour, the range being tempered by the acceptable number and mixing of the colours. It is usually most effective to use the stronger colours because, with the projection of light the weaker colours have a very washed-out appearance when they reach the screen.

Underlining, bullets, upper case/lower case, boxes, etc can all be used as effectively on the OHP slide as on the flipchart, and the transparency can be considered a miniature flipchart that will be projected to a larger size than a flipchart. Herein lies a caveat – because of the magnification of the initial image on to the screen, any faults or imperfections will also be magnified and exaggerated. So it is essential that a practised and professional approach is taken.

Size of lettering

The size of the lettering or writing on the transparency will depend on the extent to which the image will be magnified on the screen, and the size of the group and its distance from the screen. A useful rule-of-thumb is:

if the audience is:
up to 10 metres distant, the lettering should have a minimum size on the transparency of 5 mm
between 10 and 15 metres, the lettering should have a minimum size of 10 mm
between 15 and 20 metres, the lettering should have a minimum of 15mm.

These sizes can be translated into computer program font sizes as:

5 mm = 20 point   10 mm = 40 point   15 mm = 60 point

PREPARING THE TRANSPARENCY

OHP transparencies or slides can be prepared in a variety of ways – written with special pens; with dry lettering and symbols; photocopied material; photographic techniques; and computer programs.

Writing

Special marker pens are used for writing or drawing on transparency films. These are generally referred to by what has become almost a generic name even though it is the trade name used by one of the manufacturers. These 'Lumocolor pens' (manufactured by Staedtler) can be obtained in the full range of colours, with points ranging from fine to very broad, and in either a permanent, spirit-based or temporary, water-based form. The permanent markers need to be removed with spirit or a special remover; the water-based ones being removable with a damp cloth.

Permanent markers are used on slides that are to form a library of OHP visual aids designed for repeated use, and that can form part of a larger visual aid library.

Water-based markers are normally used for temporary trans-parencies completed during a session, either by the trainer making additional points or taking back feedback from learning groups, or by the learners themselves when making individual statements or summaries of group learning. These markers are usually used on acetate squares which, after the event, can be erased and reused on subsequent training events.

Care must be taken when writing or drawing freehand on a transparency, particularly with permanent markers, as unless you are particularly skilled at lettering the end result can look amateurish. On some occasions, for example when using an acetate square as a memo pad during learning group feedback, perfection is not sought, only clarity and legibility. One method of helping you to make your lettering as legible and consistent as possible is to use a paper sheet on which the lettering has been entered by, eg a computer or a typewriter, as a template, placing the acetate over the paper and tracing what is required.

However good a letterer you may be, the end result will rarely be as good as printed examples, although the use of the pens has the benefit of speed and flexibility.

Dry lettering and symbols

These are a very acceptable alternative to the use of Lumocolors and produce clear, legible, well-formed and consistent images. Such lettering is obtainable as Letraset and is used by transferring the letters or symbols, one at a time, on to the transparency film by rubbing the lettering with a pencil as the sheet containing it is placed over the acetate. The lettering sheets usually have an aid to ensure straight lines of lettering. I find it easier to have a sheet of paper with prominent lines drawn on it to use as a template. The technique produces very professional-looking slides, but their production is very time con-suming. However, when completed, they are semi-permanent slides that can be used over and over again. I say 'semi' because the heat from an OHP can tend to make the lettering lift from the film and other pressures can remove the letters or parts of them. Of course, an erased letter or symbol can be replaced, but again time and care are necessary.

Photocopying

Any material that can be photocopied can be converted easily into an OHP slide, provided the photocopier is capable of accepting trans-parent film in addition to paper – most are nowadays. The source material should be of high quality, otherwise the poorer quality will be transferred to the slide and magnified and exaggerated in the projection. Lettering and symbols should be bold to enable flexibility of reproduction – dry lettering is particularly suitable for this purpose when more than one copy is required, and the resulting slide will be more permanent than dry lettering straight on to film.

The photocopier makes the source material availability much wider, although care must be taken in deciding to use particular sources (and always remember the restrictions of copyright). Book print is not very suitable for reproduction without extensive magnification that can degrade the image, although illustrations can often be successfully reproduced. Typewritten reports are rarely successfully reproduced as the typescript is usually not clear or sufficiently large – other approaches are much better. (Figure 4.7 shows an example of repro-duced typescript).

```
                    VISUAL AIDS

            BARRIERS TO ADULT LEARNING

                Previous experience

                Lack of confidence

                Lack of motivation

                 Fear of failure

                Old dog syndrome

                Lack of interest
```

Figure 4.7 *Example of typed slide*

Similarly, avoid extensive tables of figures – these may reproduce successfully, but the end result is usually an overcrowded, unintelligible transparency full of figures: tables are usually more effectively reproduced in graphic form.

Photographic techniques

Lettering, symbols, graphics and photographs can be successfully transferred to a transparent film, suitable for transmission by an OHP, by photographic techniques. This is particularly true for photographs when their original size (eg 35mm) is not a suitable medium for communication. However, the technique usually requires a professional photographic laboratory and this can be expensive. In many cases, even the projection of photographs, the result can be achieved by other means, eg the computer.

COMPUTER TECHNIQUES FOR TRANSPARENCY PREPARATION

The computer is nowadays probably the medium used most frequently for the production of OHP slides and it has numerous advantages over other methods, not least of which is the flexibility of approach. The computer approach is particularly appropriate when permanent or very durable slides are required. Most computer programs have an almost endless range of fonts (lettering); a wide range of sizes; libraries of graphics in the form of symbols, shapes, photographs and clip-art drawings; and a range of borders or frames to suit all tasks. In fact the choice is almost bewildering and has the added danger that, because they are there, the slide producer may tend to over-use them, and so reduce the slide impact.

Choice of lettering

The first choice faced by the computer-generated transparency maker is the same one that the flipchart producer encountered – whether to use upper case, lower case or a mixture of both types of lettering in the one aid. There is little to help in this choice, whether the image is flipchart or computer generated.

The next choice also concerns lettering, and in this case, the type of lettering, there is a much wider choice and consequently a more difficult decision-making process. The initial choice here is between *serif* and *sans serif* lettering. Serif lettering has extensions to the letters – eg A, a, M, m, etc – whereas sans serif does not – eg A, a, M, m, etc. Frequently used fonts of the serif nature are *Times* and of the sans serif, *Arial*. In addition there are numerous decorative fonts such as Chaucer, Broadway, COPPERPLATE, *Brushcript*, MuralScript, and so on. However, many are too decorative to be used in transparencies that require clarity above attractiveness of appearance. But they can be used in a controlled manner, for example as striking headlines. The usual advice is either to stick to one font or use, at the most, two distinctly separate ones, and also to maintain a constant size of lettering from one slide to the next. However, I find this too restricting, and personally I feel that seeing one slide after another with the same size and the same lettering ceases to have impact, and my attention starts to take a sharp dip.

Serif v sans serif

Figures 4.8 and 4.9 reproduce an illustration I have used earlier in this book, the first with a sans serif type and the second with serif. Figure 4.10 mixes these two types with different heading and sub-heading. Which do you prefer and which do you think makes the most impact?

VISUAL AIDS   **VISUAL AIDS**

LEGIBILITY   LEGIBILITY

Clarity of writing   Clarity of writing

Quality of writing   Quality of writing

Graphics   Graphics

Use of colour   Use of colour

Use of boxes   Use of boxes

Underlining   Underlining

Aim for clarity and impact   Aim for clarity and impact

Figure 4.8 *A computer-generated*   **Figure 4.8** *A computer-generated*
slide using sans serif type   *slide using serif type*

VISUAL AIDS

LEGIBILITY

Clarity of writing

Quality of writing

Graphics

Use of colour

Use of boxes

Underlining

Aim for clarity and impact

Figure 4.10 *A computer-generated slide using both serif and
sans serif type*

Figure 4.11 demonstrates the use of the decorative fonts, in this case with the heading and subheading in *Chaucer* type and the remainder in *Black Forest*. How do you react to these?

VISUAL AIDS

LEGIBILITY

Clarity of writing

Quality of writing

Graphics

Use of colour

Use of boxes

Underlining

Aim for clarity and impact

Figure 4.11   *Mixed decorative type*

Use of borders and frames

The illustrations of visual aids reproduced here have very simple formats and include only the relevant wording or graphics. Computer-generated slides can easily have borders or frames added around the words, or can have a consistent background format. Many computer programs include these or have the facility to link parts of different applications.

The vast majority of OHP transparencies that I produce for my own use are computer generated and printed on a laser printer. I use a variety of software applications including Serif PagePlus Home/Office Edition and Mega ArtPack CD to produce the masters for these slides and print them straight on to laser-compatible film. I have other applications that contain clip-art and pictures than can be imported by these programs, so with this combination I have all I need to produce a wide range of types of slides. I have about 250 different fonts that I can use and the applications have innumerable slide formats on which

I can call. My principal difficulty is the one mentioned earlier – the problems created in choice from a superfluity of items.

Figures 4.12 and 4.13 demonstrate two of the variations that can be achieved with even the simpler approaches.

VISUAL AIDS

LEGIBILITY

Clarity of writing

Quality of writing

Graphics

Use of colour

Use of boxes

Underlining

Aim for clarity and impact

Figure 4.12 *A simple border slide*

VISUAL AIDS

LEGIBILITY

Clarity of writing

Quality of writing

Graphics

Use of colour

Use of boxes

Underlining

Aim for clarity and impact

Figure 4.13 *A double border slide*

White on black

As I have tried to demonstrate, the variety of OHP transparencies you can design and produce with the help of the computer is almost endless. This description can be concluded with a suggestion that reverses all the approaches shown so far. Figures 4.7 to 4.13 show the traditional black (or coloured) lettering on a white, transparent background: how about reversing this so that the slide has a black background with white lettering superimposed? The computer makes this reversal easy.

There is little doubt that slides of this nature are impactive, if not just different, and can have significant added value in any session. But, as usual, there is a caveat, and in this case it is that slides in this format must be used sparingly if the impact is to be maintained. Continuous exposure to this kind of slide can harm more than help, most people find them tiring when shown in quantity, with a reduction of impact. Use them but sparingly, retaining them for really key messages or items that you want to stand out in the learners' vision and minds. The learners will certainly take notice when one of these is projected among a series of traditional black-on-white slides.

If all black does not appeal to you, try a traditional slide but with some parts placed in boxes that have a black fill with white lettering, say the heading, the subheading and an impact entry. Figures 4.14 and 4.15 demonstrate these two examples of black/white usage.

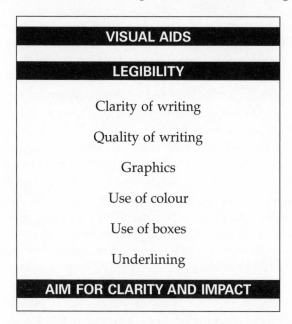

Figure 4.14 *Partial white on black slide example*

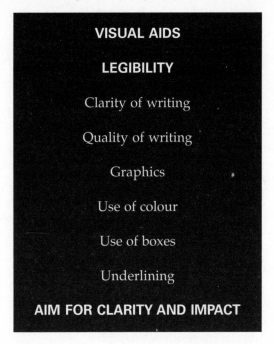

Figure 4.15 *White on black slide example*

Horizontal and vertical formats

One of the many discussions that develop when OHP slide design is being considered is concerned with the layout format; whether the slide should be in landscape (horizontal) or portrait (vertical) format. This problem does not arise with the acetate square, but A4 film, like its paper counterpart, and printers linked with computers have one long dimension and one short one; these dimensions can be manipulated into portrait or landscape format.

Arguments abound about the merits of either format, but it seems to come down to personal preference. More words per line can obviously be included on the landscape format, although with fewer lines; more lines can be included on the portrait format, but each with fewer words. I much prefer the upright format, perhaps because this is the medium in which I do almost 100 per cent of my work, and also because of my photographer experiences in which my forte was the portrait.

When you need to combine graphics and words the landscape format is usually the more effective as the two aspects can be set out clearly, although the words may need to be smaller and fewer lines may be available. Figure 4.16 demonstrates one of these combined slides.

ADVANTAGES OF THE OHP

- WIDE AVAILABILITY
- GROUP VISUAL CONTACT
- USED STANDING OR SITTING
- HIGH VISUAL IMPACT
- SCALEABLE IMAGE
- RELATIVELY CHEAP
- SMALL OBJECT PROJECTION
- PORTABLE TRANSPARENCIES
- EASY TRANSPARENCY PRODUCTION
- FLEXIBILITY OF USE

Figure 4.16   *The horizontal slide format*

Portrait or landscape format – which is your preference? Perhaps we may sometimes be influenced by the television image which is a horizontal format, but many people are offended by the TV technique that either cuts off the top of the images, or, to contain them in full, includes much superfluous material on each side.

Whichever format you prefer, consistency is generally more pleasing to the eye, and therefore more acceptable.

5

Overhead Projectors – 2

OTHER TIPS FOR SLIDE PRODUCTION

COLOUR PRINTING

If you have a colour printer the full benefits of computer-generated slides can be enjoyed, with various colours added for impact in addition to (or instead of) some of the other techniques. However, flexible colour printers are not universally available, the master can be more difficult to manipulate and the expense of production will be increased. If these factors inhibit thoughts of colour one alternative approach, albeit not 100 per cent effective, is to use outline letters and, when printed, fill in the letters with the required colours by means of coloured markers. If sufficient care is taken, it can be difficult to identify this technique on the projected slide. Figure 5.1 shows a slide with the basic lettering that can be used for this approach.

VISUAL AIDS
LEGIBILITY
Clarity of writing
Quality of writing
Graphics
Use of colour
Use of boxes
Underlining
AIM FOR CLARITY AND IMPACT

Figure 5.1   *Outline type for colour infilling*

GRAPHICS

If there is one element in which the computer-based application excels it is in the production of graphic images, other than lettering, that can be included in a transparency. These graphics, serious or humorous, can either enhance a slide or be slides in themselves, making them more interesting and acceptable to the learners.

There is a caveat, however, that, as with comedy training films, not everybody likes humour on a slide, feeling that it interferes with the serious message (this feeling is expressed by trainers and learners alike).

There are literally thousands of clip-art and photo graphics available, most now on CD-ROMs. The excellent Serif PagePlus Home/Office Edition and its supporting CD-ROMs provide many of these and they can be easily integrated with various applications to produce a novel/interesting slide.

The simplest and most useful graphics are those you custom build yourself. If you want to be adventurous with bubbles and balloons as call-outs these can be produced easily, and even aircraft producing banners and faces, etc. Figures 5.2 and 5.3 show a small selection of these.

Figure 5.2 *Call-out graphics*

When it is necessary to add an illustration to words on a slide, draw simple pictures of useful objects, or even complete illustrations, the applications mentioned can provide an image for almost whatever you may require. CD-ROMs are now available with photo images in addition to the simpler clip-art, and these too can be reproduced as part of or as a complete slide.

Figure 5.3   *Clip-art graphics*

GRAPHS AND CHARTS

It is difficult to reproduce masses of figures and numbers on a slide, principally because they are difficult for the viewer to assimilate, even with, or because of, accompanying verbal descriptions by the trainer or presenter. Few visual aids are themselves explicit enough to stand alone without description and, as we have seen, this is not their purpose. But when we reach the stage that the presenter has to stop to explain the visual aid intended to support the presentation, then something has gone wrong with the aid.

This usually occurs when charts, graphs and diagrams are shown and the presenter wants to make them as comprehensive as possible. The end result is often a slide crammed with too much information for the viewer to take in. The advice must be, as with the spoken and written word, KISS.

Tabulated data

Data to be presented visually is usually obtained from tables contained in reports. The naive may think that the most effective way of showing this data is to reproduce the table – in this way, all the data is there and all the presenter has to do is to:

1. display the data for the members to read
2. explain the data – what it is, where it came from, etc
3. explain the analyses of the data.

Table 5.1 shows the number of unit trusts arranged during a ten-year period.

Table 5.1 *Unit trust purchases*

	Millions of currency units			
Year	**Ordinary**	**Special**	**Complex**	**Total**
1970	104,883	29,169	12,888	146,940
1971	110,322	34,088	14,000	158,410
1972	113,992	31,066	14,092	159,150
1973	128,534	36,304	14,308	179,146
1974	148,024	47,468	14,624	210,116
1975	186,970	47,170	14,592	248,732
1976	187,386	52,438	14,156	253,980
1977	189,388	61,636	14,102	265,126
1978	207,888	72,954	13,348	294,190
1979	227,000	78,658	12,908	318,566
1980	245,960	94,006	13,210	353,176
Totals	1,850,347	584,957	152,228	2,587,532

If you wished to use this data on an OHP or 35 mm slide in the form of the table itself, very little benefit would result. The problems are that:

- there is too much detail to be included in one projected slide
- breaking the table into several slides would make description and comparison too difficult
- the image is one of many large figures that dissolve into each other and make the eyes glaze over
- if the learners are not fully conversant with the data they cannot be expected to analyse the figures from this mass of information suddenly presented to them.

You are then faced with two problems to solve.

1. Which aspects of analysis do I want and/or need to demonstrate?
2. Which method of presentation is going to be the most effective for this kind of data, ie what form of visual aid?

Among other factors, the table demonstrates change. The horizontal totals show the change of the monetary value of purchases of unit trusts over 11 years; the vertical totals show the relative size of purchases between ordinary, special and complex unit trusts. Both these aspects can be compared in a visual aid.

In addition, the relative sizes of purchases of the three types of trust can be compared in each year; each figure can be converted to a percentage of its own column, its own year or full totals of the decade or the type of trust.

Any or all of these can be converted from the table to a visual aid, and a further choice of the style of visual aid becomes available.

CHART FORMS

Any information can be presented in the form of a 'chart', a description commonly used for a range of charts, diagrams, drawings, etc, each one being most effective when used for a particular purpose. The charts in most common use, and described here, include pie, bar, column and line charts and graphs.

Pie charts

A pie chart is a circle divided into segments, each segment showing a relative-sized part of the whole. Because all the information is included in the one circle the pie chart is ideally suited to showing at a glance a comparison of the components.

However, bearing Table 5.1 in mind, the value of the pie would be destroyed if too many components were included; the pie is at its best with six or so components.

Positioning the components can be important. The eye is used to moving in a clockwise direction and to do so starts at about the 12 or 1 o'clock positions. It may therefore be appropriate to place the segment that contains the most important information in this position, although this is not necessarily essential if the segments are clearly indicated.

The segments will be graded in size according to the size of the component being compared. If this can be produced accurately, this should be done, otherwise, although approximate sizes can be used, these should still demonstrate the relative differences in size.

Colours or shadings can be used to differentiate between segments, although this is not completely essential as a line divides each segment. However, shading of some nature makes the segmentation more obvious.

Do not place labels inside the segments of the chart; always keep them outside the chart.

Figure 5.4 gives an example of two pie charts with information extracted from Table 5.1. In the first (Figure 5.4a) the comparison is a simple one of the three components showing the total purchases of each type of unit in 1970. Ordinary units are 104,883 currency units = 71 per cent; special units are 29,169 = 20 per cent; complex units are 12,888 = 9 per cent.

Figure 5.4(b) violates the suggestion that the optimum division of a pie is six or so components. However, in this case, the inclusion of the 11 year segments is not too excessive to make the chart unreadable.

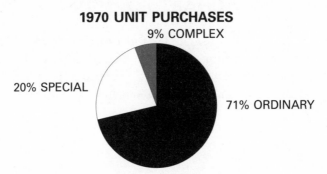

Figure 5.4a *A standard pie chart*

Figure 5.4b *A standard pie chart (multidivision)*

A number of variations on the standard pie chart are possible, the most useful and most frequently used being the exploded pie chart. In this version, the segment representing the component that the presenter wishes to make prominent is separated from the remainder of the pie.

The separated segment can be at any place in the pie and prominence is helped if the segment is positively shaded. Figure 5.5 is a representation of an exploded pie chart, again using the figures from our original table.

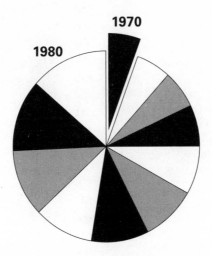

Figure 5.5 *An exploded pie chart*

Bar charts

Pie charts have the advantage of being relatively simple to construct; they need not be accurately drawn and can present simple information in an impactive manner. Another advantage is that they rarely have to be drawn by hand – every computer, however simple, has a software graphics program that enables pie charts to be constructed easily. Similar comments apply to virtually all the methods of presenting charts, so you have no argument for not using these.

But pie charts, because of their simplicity, cannot show the finer details. Of course, captions can be placed alongside or within a segment giving information, but this starts to complicate the representation and make it unclear.

A chart which is useful in describing changes and comparisons in rather more detail is the bar or column chart. In its standard form it consists of a graph, but instead of depicting points on the graph as in a line graph, each component is described with a block or bar. The chart can have one or two detailed dimensions. In Figure 5.6 the total purchases are plotted against the amount of money involved. In its simpler form the money vertical dimension would be omitted, only the height of the bar showing the differences between the years.

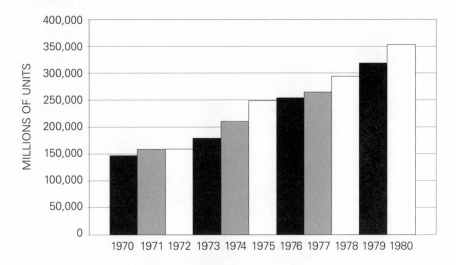

Figure 5.6 *Vertical bar chart*

The bar chart in Figure 5.6 is presented with the bars vertical. This is the most frequently used method of drawing a bar chart, but many people consider it more effective if it is drawn so that the bars project horizontally from the left side vertical.

The data from Figure 5.6 is reproduced in Figure 5.7 but in the horizontal format. The space below each bar in the vertical approach is strictly limited, particularly if there are an appreciable number of bars. In the horizontal version, much more text can be added, written if necessary within the bars or, if space has been left between each bar, in that space. With simple information, such as the year in our example, additional space is not necessary so the vertical bar is satisfactory.

Line charts

The immediate reaction on the part of most people when a chart is suggested as a means of describing numerical data is to think of a graph. Line charts or graphs consist of information plotted on the vertical and horizontal axes with a point placed at the intersection of these axes. The points are then joined by a continuous straight or curved line.

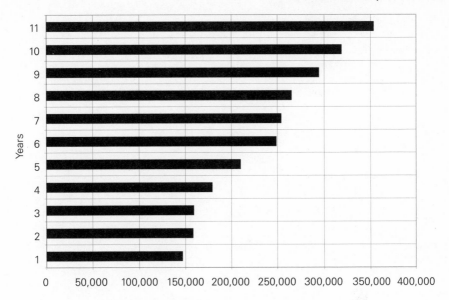

Figure 5.7 *Simple horizontal bar chart*

Some simple rules can be followed to ensure that the chart is as clear as possible. Usually the vertical scale represents magnitude or level and the horizontal scale time. The stages should be consistent in size and continuity – if some data is missing a space should be left rather than ignoring its absence; otherwise the trends will be distorted.

There is no need to start the vertical scale always at zero; this can throw all the information into the top part of the graph, thus losing impact. Instead start with a scale point one step lower than the first point or with the first point at the intersection of the vertical and horizontal axes.

Graph constructors must always be aware of possible distortions introduced by using scales that are inconsistent with the information range – variable scale steps, omitted steps and exaggerated scales all manipulate the appearance of the graph and contaminate the visual impression. (These distortions are frequently used to attempt to give false impressions and can often be successful – political presentations are frequently perpetrators of this deception.)

Figure 5.8 is a typical line graph with the points joined by straight lines – the easiest although not always the best way of joining the points. In this case, the yearly totals of all units purchased are plotted against their monetary values.

Showing the changing factors of a number of components, for example the growth of each of the unit trust types, can cause problems in the vertical size of the graph. In the case of the units, there is a large

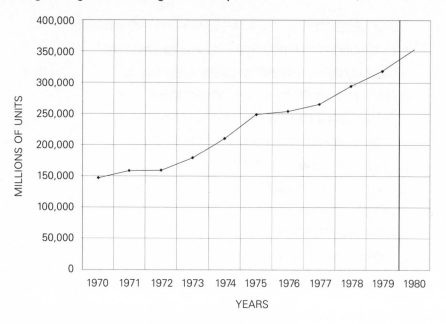

Figure 5.8 *A line graph*

variation in the levels – the low-level complex figures are close to the base of the graph with a large gap to the figures for the ordinary units at the top of the graph. On occasions this can be avoided by having two vertical scales for two components, one at the left, the other at the right. This works with two components, but with multiple cases it may be more appropriate to use another medium, for example a bar or column chart. However, in spite of the non-aesthetic nature of the multiple line graph with wide differences, these very differences may show the significance of the comparison between the components. Figure 5.9 demonstrates this. Use four or five lines at most on the graph, otherwise there can be confusion; differently-coloured lines will help to minimize this. Avoid, wherever possible, vertical labels on the X (vertical) axis that are difficult to read – use horizontal labels even if these reduce the graph size to some extent.

The principal variation in the line graph is the replacement of the straight lines joining the points by a line curving to follow the direction of the next point. This produces a pleasant image and a more accurate demonstration of the movement, but requires good draughtsmanship to ensure these aspects.

There are of course numerous other types of charts, and if the pie, bar or line charts do not satisfy your particular needs, you will need to

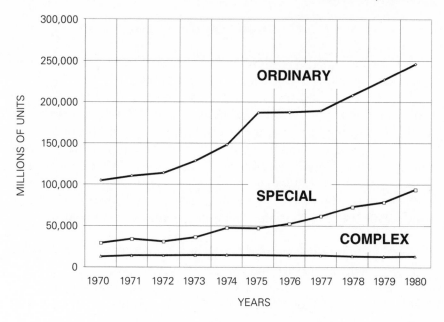

Figure 5.9 *A multicomponent line graph*

refer to one of the specialist books on the subject. But remember that the more complex the chart the more difficult it is for the audience to understand easily, and the more explanation you will have to give. Again bear in mind KISS!

TECHNIQUES FOR USING OHP SLIDES

There are two basic OHP techniques, and these are the same as for the flipchart – the additive and the subtractive, disclosure or reveal. However, there are several variations within each technique that are either impossible or very difficult with other aids.

ADDITIVE TECHNIQUES

There are three useful methods that can be used in this technique:

1. addition during the session
2. overlays
3. disclosure or reveal.

Addition during the session

This technique has been described fully for the flipchart and was mentioned in the previous chapter. It consists of starting simply with a blank transparency, writing on this, usually with a Lumocolor, to make the points you wish to highlight or to take feedback comments from the learning group(s). Acetate squares or other film can be used for this purpose, the pens being water based so that the writing can be erased when no longer needed, thus allowing the slide to be used again. The advantage of this technique with the OHP compared with the flipchart is the common one with OHPs, namely that you are in constant touch with the group, facing them all the time, even when you are writing.

A refinement or variation of this approach (possible only with ease with the OHP) avoids having to add other transparencies when one has been used. If a continuous roll of acetate film is attached to the OHP, when the part of the roll over the platen is used it is simple to wind on to the next blank area. This facilitates backwards and forwards reference to material, but can become complicated if some distance separates the material.

Perhaps it was a little gimmicky, but I have used a prepared roll at the end of a training event to show a goodbye message, with relevant graphics and accompanied by appropriate music! There are numerous other applications if you have this facility.

Overlays

The use of overlays avoids having an overcrowded single slide, particularly important when starting to describe a process or other area of learning. There are several ways of producing overlays – some are easier and some more effective in particular circumstances than others. However, the basic starting point is common to all methods – start with a blank acetate or one with a simple entry, usually the starting point of a build up. For example, if you are going to describe an electric plug, the first sheet might contain an outline of the body of the plug. To this first transparency other sheets are added progressively, building up to the completed slide which might consist of three or four sheets.

Figure 5.10 demonstrates a set of five parts to produce the final projection (6).

This approach demands the exact registration of each transparency with the others. One method is to mount each slide accurately on a card frame; these are then placed exactly one on top of each other as

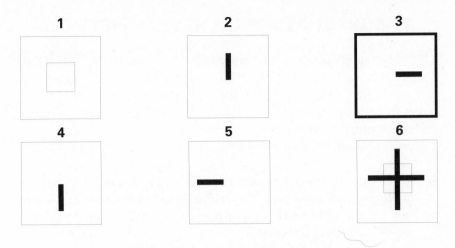

Figure 5.10   *The additive method*

the build up progresses. This method works, but there is the danger of the top layer being slightly out of focus as the depth of focus of the OHP lens is not very large. The card frames can be omitted and registration marks placed on each transparency to guide placement. These marks can be unobtrusively placed outside the projected area of the transparency, but you might sometimes be excessively involved in ensuring exact registration.

A more effective method, and certainly one that avoids having to take risks with manual registration, is to fix the unmounted transparencies to the sides of the first, card-mounted transparency with adhesive tape. The other transparencies start folded away from the platen and are folded over as needed. The transparencies can all be fixed on one side, one above the other but, with the tendency of acetate films to curl, this can produce problems when they are folded over. One-side fixing also makes the use of the slides inflexible, which may not be a problem. Flexibility can be introduced by fixing the transparencies to different sides of the original frame and folding them over as required. *Make sure that you number each transparency!*

Unfortunately, a composite slide of this nature can look messy with the transparencies hanging over the sides, and with an OHP with a strong cooling fan they can wave about until folded over the platen. However, if this is the most appropriate approach for that particular slide and event, these negative factors can be ignored.

Another option, useful when an image has to be built up horizontally or vertically in stages, is to fix rectangles of film, rather than full sheets, to the sides of the initial frame and fold these over as and when required. This is a very flexible method.

THE DISCLOSURE OR REVEAL METHOD

This is the method that is probably in most common use with OHP users, particularly the simple, single sheet method. With a slide (such as that shown in Figure 4.12) on the OHP platen, place a sheet of A4 paper or card over it, and move the card down as you want to reveal each item progressively.

This technique has two problems:

1. When you approach the bottom of the slide the card is in danger of slipping off the top of the OHP, as most of it overhangs – you can put a weight on the upper part of the card to avoid this, but this is rather unprofessional.
2. Unless you know the slide contents well, until you move the card to reveal the next item you do not know what it is.

Both these problems can be avoided by the simple expedient of placing the paper or card *under* the transparency rather than on top. In this way you can still reveal the material progressively and always be fully aware of the slide content. Figure 5.11 demonstrates this technique.

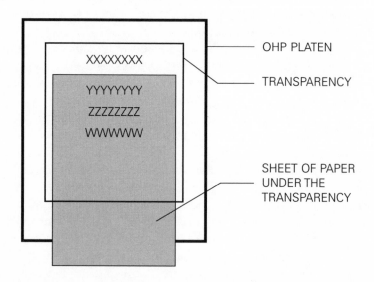

Figure 5.11 *Revealing with a sheet of paper/card*

The weight of the transparency, particularly if it is mounted on a card frame, will be sufficient to stop the paper from slipping even when the lower parts of the slide are concerned.

Even more flexibility is introduced if special disclosure masks are made when these are appropriate. If, for example the slide includes four themes, each of these can be placed in a quarter of the slide – exact quartering is not necessary. Four card masks sufficiently large to cover each quarter separately are fixed to the sides of the slide frame with adhesive tape so that they can be folded away from the part of the slide as required. The identity of the hidden parts can be written on the covering cards. Figure 5.12 demonstrates this approach.

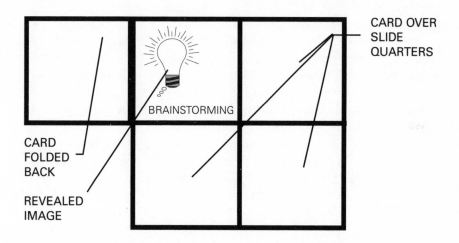

Figure 5.12   *Slide reveal method with card masks*

As with virtually any method or technique, overuse of the disclosure method, particularly a long slide with a lot of items to be disclosed, can become irritating to the viewing group. Although disclosure avoids a lot of possible problems it may be advisable to give full disclosure sometimes.

SOME USEFUL OHP PRACTICES

Some tips have been given throughout this and the preceding chapter for using the OHP to maximum effectiveness, eg avoiding keystoning, screen visibility, writing techniques. Here are some more general ones.

Framing

Having a transparency mounted on an OHP card frame has been mentioned several times previously. This is usually very good practice, as it:

- helps to keep the transparency in good condition
- assists handling what can sometimes be a slippery piece of film
- allows notes and 'stage directions' to be written on the frame.

However, they make the transparency bulkier than unmounted film and consequently more difficult to store and carry, particularly if you have a large stock of them. They are, of course, safer when framed.

The transparency itself can be fixed to the frame with staples – ensure that the 'open' ends are facing up to avoid damage to the lens and flattened to avoid damage to fingers – or fixed around the edges by adhesive tape. Always attach the transparency to the underside of the frame to ensure close contact between the film and the lens – a gap (particularly with some portable OHPs which, because of small depth of focus) can produce unclear images or ghosting.

Filing and referencing

Always protect your transparencies, both when filed and not in use and, at the very least, when you are transporting them. A number of different transparent, plastic sleeves are produced into which the slide can be slipped in and out easily. Some have 'flip' sides on which notes about the transparency can be written.

With framed or unframed transparencies always have a heading entry on the slide itself. When the slide is framed always annotate the frame with the title and, if relevant, with notes identifying the event during which the slide will be used. In both cases an identity number can be prominently marked (although this must not defeat flexibility) on the transparency itself or the frame, in the same way that pages of a training brief are numbered. These numbers can also be indexed in your trainer's guide. This may seem to produce a lot of work, but the alternative may be to search through tens or hundreds of slides.

If you are a new trainer you will have only a few transparencies, but as your experience grows, so will your slide collection! The time will come when you will spend an excessive amount of time trying to find the slides you want. This can obviously be avoided by having an effective filing system. A variety of systems exist and you may want to experiment to see which one suits your way of working. Keep the slides separate from your briefs unless a set of slides will be used with one set of briefs only. Otherwise have a simple method of annotation with which you can identify the folder in which the slides you want are kept.

A frequently used method is to have a slide number that contains an abbreviation for the course title (eg PRES for Presentation skills; NEG for Negotiation skills; IPS for Interpersonal skills and so on), the number of the session in the course, followed by the number of the slide in the sequence used in the session (this will be annotated on the brief itself). For example, for some slides you might have:

PRES 1/1
PRES 1/2
PRES 2/1, etc.

If a slide is also used during another course a cross reference can be made with an additional entry after the main one. For example, the first slide in the first session of your IPS course that is also the 4th slide in the second session of your Negotiation skills course would be:

IPS 1/1 (NEG 2/4)

When you have multiple use slides there should also be a note in the brief about where the slide is held, for example NEG 2/4 (IPS1/1).

It is useful also to have a consistent reference format for other session documents such as handouts, activity briefs, etc.

Pointing

When you want to point to a projected item from an OHP slide, point at the slide on the OHP, not at the screen. Do so in a positive manner, rather than with a vague wave. Use the pointed end of a pencil, or a small stick with a pointed end, and when you point to the slide place the point end *on the slide*, rather than hovering above it, since your hand and the pointer will inevitably shake. An alternative is to lay the pointer down on top of the slide with the point at the part you wish to highlight. If you do this, use a non-rounded pencil or pointer otherwise there will be a tendency for it to roll off the slide. Placing the pointer on the slide leaves both your hands free for other purposes. Or why not make a small, solid flat arrow pointer in wood or card?

Overtalking

Don't talk over the start of a slide projection. When you first illuminate the slide, wait a few seconds before you start talking to allow the group to become accustomed to the change from your talking to the visual object.

Handouts

Whether you ask the learners to or not, many will be taking notes as you speak and show your training aids. It is difficult for them to look, listen, analyse and write at the same time, so as far as your visual aids are concerned:

- tell the learners you have copies of the slides for them
- ensure you make copies of the aids or have handouts made from them.

When you are considering using slide copies and handouts, do not just think of one slide:one handout – you can save paper and ease reference and learning by shrinking the slide copy so that, say, four slides are accommodated on one page. If you use heavy grade paper both sides can be used effectively.

OHPs and their slides, etc are probably the most flexible and useful training aid that is readily available to almost every trainer and presenter – use them and use them creatively. Impactive, interesting, enjoyable training aids will assist learning more than any other approach.

A FINAL CHECK OF YOUR OHP SLIDE

1. Produce a slide that you feel contains the material you wish to project during your session.
2. Project the slide (or one part of it if it contains several parts that will be disclosed progressively). Read the content of the projected image and time this reading.
3. If the reading exceeds five to ten seconds there is too much material and it needs editing.
4. Does the material *support* your input, or does it merely repeat what you are saying? If the latter, edit the material to appear as key words or phrases only.
5. Project the slide again and check its visibility from all parts of the training room.

6
—
Other Projectors

Other projectors, albeit not as common as the OHP, are used in training and development presentations. Suitable for a range of operations, they include:

■ episcopes
■ OHP projection equipment
■ 35mm slide projectors and allied equipment.

EPISCOPES

Episcopes are not often encountered nowadays, which is unfortunate, as they can be most useful pieces of equipment for particular purposes. They differ from OHPs in that, instead of projecting transparency images, they project images of solid objects, such as illustrated pages. The episcope is the modern equivalent of the older epidiascope, and consists basically of a light box with an internal platen on which the object is placed and illuminated with a strong projector bulb. The image is transmitted via a mirror through a lens on to a screen in much the same way as the OHP. The projected image is not as strongly illuminated, however, as with the OHP and consequently the episcope must be used in a darkened room. This, of course, almost completely reduces the eye contact between the trainer and the learning group, and a darkened room can have a soporific effect – particularly after lunch.

In a similar way to the OHP, the episcope has a limited depth of focus and copes more effectively with plane objects rather than those with strong three-dimensional proportions. Book pages are particularly easy to project, whether pages of words or illustrations – line drawings are preferable to half-tone photographs as the tones can tend to fuse into similar shades. Another advantage of the episcope over the OHP is that the former reproduces the projected object in its original colours without the need for any manipulation as we saw with the OHP transparency.

The facility of the OHP for projecting slides on to a flipchart and the tracing of this projected image to produce a large graphic was mentioned earlier. The episcope can be employed in the same way, but without the need to produce a transparency. The illustration can be projected directly on to the flipchart and a tracing made which can then be line marked and colour filled as required. This graphic, which can be a strong image in full colour, reproduced almost exactly as the original, is sufficiently large to be photographed easily if a 35 mm slide is required. This projected image is extremely versatile, the size being easily adjustable, colours introduced, and annotations made as required.

The advantages and disadvantages are summarized in Figure 6.1.

```
+--------------------------------------------------+
|                   ADVANTAGES                     |
|                                                  |
|    ■  PROJECTS SOLID OBJECTS AS IMAGES           |
|       ■  REPRODUCES ORIGINAL COLOURS             |
|                ■  VERSATILE                       |
|            ■  PROJECTED IMAGE                     |
+--------------------------------------------------+
```

```
+--------------------------------------------------+
|                  DISADVANTAGES                   |
|                                                  |
|            ■  NEEDS DARKENED ROOM                |
|     ■  REDUCED EYE CONTACT WITH GROUP            |
|         ■  LIMITED DEPTH OF FOCUS                |
+--------------------------------------------------+
```

Figure 6.1   *Advantages and disadvantages of the episcope*

THE VIDEO OHP

The video OHP can be more correctly called in some versions the 'video episcope', as it uses solid objects rather than transparencies for its projection subjects. Figure 6.2 shows this piece of equipment diagrammatically: a video camera (A) takes the place of the OHP mirror and lens head and the baseboard (B) is just that rather than the light box and Fresnel Lens. Instead of the light source being inside a box, as in the case of the OHP, illumination is provided by light sources (C) usually placed on each side of the baseboard/platen.

The image recorded by the video camera is then transmitted to a monitor on which the original object is clearly displayed, and in full colour (depending on the monitor). The advantage of this piece of equipment is that objects with a greater depth can be projected compared with the standard OHP and the episcope. Also, of course, the projection is not limited to static objects, the video camera being capable of recording movement, whether in-built or produced by rotating the object to demonstrate different angles.

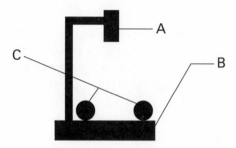

Figure 6.2   *The video OHP*

Two disadvantages are apparent. The first concerns price. The equipment is costly compared with the standard OHP or episcope – for example, in early 1998 in the UK a deluxe model, with many added features, retailed for more than £4,000.

The second disadvantage can be avoided with the use of another piece of equipment. A television monitor is relatively small and therefore suitable only for quite small audiences. It is therefore necessary, for larger groups, to project a considerably larger image. This is effected through another piece of equipment that is variously described as a multimedia projector, an LCD projector or large screen projector, but basically it takes a video image and, instead of displaying this directly on a monitor, projects a full-colour image on to a large screen. The video projector is linked to the video OHP and projects a full-colour image. Early models were difficult to set up, requiring fine balancing of the three principal colours of a video-produced image, but current models have a much simpler setting-up facility. Such projectors currently retail from £7,000, but offer considerable flexibility for realism and projection under the most difficult lighting conditions. See Figure 6.3.

Figure 6.3 *A large-screen projector*

One advantage of video OHPs, whether or not they need to be linked to large-screen projectors, is that they require little or no preparation of the material to be viewed – a book; an illustration; an object, whether static or movable/moving, etc – place the item on the platen and the image is projected in full reality.

The advantages and disadvantages are summarized in Figure 6.4.

This equipment has other uses in the training aid field and these will be referred to later.

ADVANTAGES

NO NEED FOR DARKENED ROOM

LITTLE OR NO MATERIAL PREPARATION

PROJECTS SOLID OBJECTS AS IMAGES

PROJECTS STATIC AND NON-STATIC
OBJECTS AS IMAGES

DISADVANTAGES

COSTLY TO PURCHASE

CAN BE DIFFICULT TO SET UP

Figure 6.4 *Advantages and disadvantages of the video OHP*

35 mm SLIDE PROJECTORS AND ALLIED EQUIPMENT

The training aid material and equipment that is most effective in producing realistic reproductions and projections of training items is the photographic slide (commonly 35 mm), projected through a slide projector produced for this purpose. See Figure 6.5.

The slides can be commercially produced, custom made by professional organizations or even produced by experienced photographers within a company.

Figure 6.5   *The photographic slide projector*

Advantages

- Once the slides have been produced they are easily stored, easily transported and easily used.
- The slides can be produced in extremely high quality and in full, natural colour – both this advantage and the preceding one need not be expensive, although complex photographic techniques can be costly.
- Natural scenes, objects, line diagrams, etc can all be shown with little problem.
- The photographs can be taken by almost anyone with almost any camera, although obviously the more skilled the photographer and the higher the quality of the equipment, the higher the quality of the end product.
- Sets of slides can be easily made up and readied for projection.

Disadvantages

- Black-out is necessary to enable the projected images to be viewed with clarity and ease, thus losing the trainer-learner eye contact and making it difficult for the learners to make notes. There is also the potentially soporific effect mentioned earlier.

- The method is less flexible than the OHP, particularly now that most slide projectors use slide carousels in which the slides are placed prior to the presentation. It is of course possible to move backwards and forwards to desired slides, but there must be an easy way of identifying the required slide.
- Black- or white-out between slides can be very distracting and annoying. It is possible to avoid this with linking slides between each one in the set, or using two linked projectors with a fade facility.
- There is the potential problem of slides jamming, with the consequent breakdown in the flow of the session.

SLIDE PREPARATION

Considerable care should be taken to produce the highest quality slides for projection. Photographs of scenes and places have the least flexibility, although, unless the need is pressing, you can await optimum conditions. Objects, unless we are considering large machinery *in situ*, are usually photographed under studio conditions where lighting, backcloths, etc can all be arranged. Similar remarks apply to slides made of posters, such as those used in OHP projection, and in fact projected images of these can be copied by the camera, or the master can be used.

All the considerations mentioned for OHP transparencies need to be taken into account for photographic slides, and even greater care must be taken in view of the cost-permanency of the photo slide. Backgrounds, colour, special effects, lettering, layout, etc must all be considered and the OHP transparency 'rules' also apply. There are some differences, however, of which you or your slide producer should be aware.

- Slide format should be consistent: horizontal and vertical formats should not be mixed – apart from this mix not appealing to viewers, it can produce problems with projected image size. When the image is adjusted to fit vertically on the screen, a lot of space is left on each side. When the image is adjusted for a horizontal position, a lot of space must be left above and below the image to cater for vertical images. Both these effects reduce the potential size of the projected image and do not use the technique to maximum effect. Consistent format can ensure that the image is adjusted for optimum size and visibility.

- Black background slides with white or coloured images can be very impactive, but in the same way that we found with OHP slides, these should be used with care to avoid annoyance or over-familiarity.
- Colour schemes are so easily produced with photographic slides that care must be taken and certain 'rules' observed: yellow on white, blue on green, pink on red, or a rainbow selection should be avoided, not just for their non-aesthetic effect, but also because these combinations of colours are difficult to see.
- Take care with reproducing from printed lettering and pictures, particularly when enlargement is going to be great. Many of these are produced by patterns of dots which will show up with the enlargement.
- Although photographic slides can be used effectively, use slides with words only in a limited way – there are cheaper ways of producing 'word' slides, but the photo slide is supreme for graphics and cartoons.

Remember that camera work is not the only method of producing slides of this nature – some computer programs linked with special photographic processes can achieve the same results.

Back projection

The problem of darkening the room can also be minimized by the use of back projection, although this does require:

- a special screen
- additional space behind the screen
- some means of operating the slide projector remotely – there should be no major problems with modern equipment.

With this technique the slide projector is placed behind a semi-opaque screen and the slide is projected on to the rear of the screen. Because of the qualities of the screen, which usually include an enhancement facility, the projected image can be viewed easily from in front of the screen. Back projection screens do not require complete black-out for an acceptable image but the space behind the screen must be sufficient to allow a projected image of the required size. Even this does not necessarily limit the technique too greatly: a range of lens is available for the projector from wide angle to long focus. In back projection, with the limited space that is usually available, a relatively wide-angle lens is required.

A 'mini' advantage, although one that can be quickly negated because of projector problems, is that the projector is not within the body of the learning group. Front projection usually means that the projector has to be set back within the group, as opposed to the frontal position of an OHP, and, unless the trainer is equipped with a remote control his or her presence beside the projector is necessary. We cannot ignore the fact that projectors do go wrong and slides do become jammed: if this occurs, the trainer must disappear behind the screen to perform the necessary repairs.

OTHER SLIDE ADVANTAGES

In addition to the general advantages described above, photographic slides have other, more aesthetic advantages.

- Once collected into a set the slides can be used for a large number of similar sessions, being updated as necessary this advantage also applies to the additional cost of their production.
- Photographic slides, especially in a darkened room and with a powerful projector, can be projected for a very large audience using a large screen for long-range visibility.
- The slides can be of very high quality, which is frequently expected by viewers. Remote control or back projection can be easily arranged to avoid disturbing the group.

7
_

Audio and Video

A substantial and significant area of training aids involves the use of both audio and video equipment, and of course a combination of both. These include:

- AUDIO AIDS
- COMPACT DISCS
- COMBINED AUDIO-SLIDE PRESENTER
- VIDEO
- INTERACTIVE VIDEO AND CD-I

AUDIO AIDS

The audio cassette player-recorder is the electric/electronic training aid that, along with the film projector, has been used in training and development for the longest period. It preceded video and computer equipment that to a large extent have superseded it.

Uses

The cassette recorder (the common description) has a number of uses in training and development, including:

- recording in the audio medium presentations, interviews, group discussions, etc
- playing back the recorded events so that they can be interrupted at feedback points
- playing commercially recorded presentations or training sessions
- playing talks, etc recorded from the radio.

Recording

The most frequent use of the cassette recorder nowadays will be in situations where video recording equipment is either not available or the environment is not suitable. Practice interviews, presentations, negotiations and similar activities are suitable events during which to use cassette recorders with effect. The recording is particularly valuable when the event is being reviewed with the participants, who may or may not also have had observers. Feedback points can be made about significant events using the recording and any disagreement with the observers' views clarified by a replay of the relevant part.

The principal participant in, say, a counselling interview practice can be given the cassette recording, plus even the recorded feedback, to take away from the training event and review, perhaps even on their car's cassette player on their way home. Training in telephone techniques and customer care on the phone is particularly relevant for audio recording. Special telephone equipment is readily available, and it is often salutary for learners to hear what they sound like on the telephone – sometimes quite different from their face-to-face voice and revealing inflection and accent peculiarities.

Pre-recorded tapes

Pre-recorded tapes are widely available from commercial sources in a range of subjects; recordings are also available at many conferences and seminars of the contributions made by some of the speakers, either live or pre-recorded. It is not usual for these tapes to be used during training itself, although excerpts can be used to support or reinforce the trainers' comments. Instead, they are very useful as part of a self-instructional process and can be listened to in a variety of circumstances – sitting at home, at a learning desk, and even in the car travelling between home and work or out and about on business. A recording can be useful as a rehearsal reminder when travelling to an important presentation, sales visit or negotiation. Recordings of this nature replayed in the car can, almost subliminally, remind you of key points, useful phrases and major parts of the arguments.

Recorded messages from the Chairman or Chief Executive can be played at appropriate events; brief explanations or other interventions to support the trainer can be recorded by experts in particular subjects or people who are unable to attend the event, but whose contribution is essential. Examples of good and/or bad interventions, and use of comments can be pre-recorded for playback at an appropriate point as a change from the trainer's input; examples of advertising, slogans, announcements and so on can all be valuable uses of the cassette recorder.

Another source of material that can be used during a session to support or reinforce the trainer, can be talks on the radio – be careful of copyright and broadcasting restrictions with these, however.

In general, then, audio recordings can be useful and helpful, but use them sparingly. People nowadays are more accustomed to and responsive to visual productions than purely audio ones.

Music

A final useful application of audio recordings is not always directly as a training aid, but in the wider application of helping to make the training event interesting and acceptable. If you are holding a training course that will be starting at a specific time in a specific place, you can be certain that the participants will not all arrive together only a few minutes before the starting time. Rather, individuals will start coming to the training room from at least 15 minutes before the due time. If they all know each other there are few problems as they will start talking together quite happily. But if they are strangers to each other there will be a certain amount of unease and nervousness: the 'strange' atmosphere can often be improved by playing suitable music in the background, thus avoiding the dreaded silence. Not everybody will appreciate this, but my experience is that more do than not. But don't play heavy rock, heavy metal or very loud music of any kind; a low level, popular classical music, perhaps Baroque, should be generally acceptable. Similarly, during lunch breaks, coffee intervals, evening study or activity periods, background music can help to make the atmosphere less of a formal training environment. It is, useful, however, to keep a check with the participants about their views on the music, as this background noise is often associated with annoying, permanent 'musak' pervading a hotel or restaurant.

Microphones

The advantage of the audio recorder over the video camera is that it is a much less obvious piece of equipment, with consequently less notice being taken by the participants in, say, a practice interview. The necessary microphone can be the only obvious evidence that the equipment exists and, even with these, current models are so sensitive that they do not need to be near the speaker(s). The quality of the recorder will normally be in direct ratio to the amount of money it costs – more expensive systems will be more sensitive, have more complex functions, will have more lifelike playback facilities, and so on. Many of these functions, unless you are making a professional recording, will just get in the way. A clear recording is all that is necessary for, say, playback to the participants in a practice interview. Useful, however, are graphic equalizers that can be used to adjust the sound input and output to ensure that bad acoustics are taken account of as far as possible.

The quality of microphones can vary considerably and poor quality ones can make a considerable difference to the sound quality. Some microphones have a very concentrated cone within which they receive sound, others a very wide receiving cone. Use the most appropriate one for the particular event and the best quality possible will be obtained. The use of multimicrophone set-ups can improve the received signals when there is more than one participant involved – for example, in a practice interview a highly directional microphone for each participant will produce excellent quality. Mixers can be used although this equipment usually requires somebody to operate it. If the trainer is available for this there is then no problem, but this is not always possible, so perhaps simple multientry microphones will be sufficient.

Figure 7.1 shows these two approaches in simple graphic form.

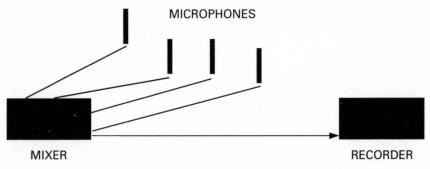

Figure 7.1a   *Multimicrophone mixer set-up*

Figure 7.1b   *Twin-microphone simple set-up*

Finally, as far as cassette recorders (however simple or complex) are concerned, make sure by specific checks before the event that the equipment is in *perfect*, not just acceptable working order, and that you have all the necessary tapes in good condition. Even with this thorough preparation remember that you are dealing with delicate electric and electronic equipment that has an infinite capacity for going wrong at the most inopportune times!

COMPACT DISCS

Developments in technology are always happening and the audio field is well represented. The major audio advance in recent years is the introduction of the compact disc, or CD. The CD can reproduce the spoken word or music at a much higher quality level than the standard audio tapes, even those of higher quality. The CD player (see Figure 7.2) is itself much more compact and portable than the cassette player-recorder and can also be battery or mains operated.

Figure 7.2   *The CD player*

Consequently, the CD can be used in almost every way that pre-recorded audio tapes can be used. Unfortunately, the parallel is not yet complete, although the next few years should see tremendous strides in this development. There are some CD recording capabilities available outside the professional recording studio, but these are expensive. In general, therefore, you will be restricted to professionally produced CDs – this limits their use considerably at the present time in training and development events, although developments are always taking place. Watch this space!

SYCHRONIZED TAPE-SLIDE PRESENTERS

One method of introducing a greater interest and variety into either tape playings or slide shows is to combine the two to produce a tape-slide presentation, the slides being accompanied by an interesting account, or even appropriate background music. With simple equipment – separate cassette players and slide projectors – it is possible to produce such a presentation, but you will need to change the slides either manually or by remote control. When using an automatic slide change, provided you have timed your pre-recording accurately, the set-up can be virtually left alone to operate. However, repeating the caveat of the ever-present possibility of component failure, you would be wise to stay nearby. The major problem will not be any breakdown of the equipment itself, but related problems when you start up again. If the slides have jammed, the recorder will have continued for a little time until you could stop it. When you restart you have, in the case of the spoken word on tape, to resynchronize the tape recorder and the slide projector – not always an easy task.

Many of these problems and difficulties can be avoided by some form of electronically controlled and synchronized tape-slide equipment. It is relatively simple and inexpensive to attach a piece of electronic equipment between the tape recorder and the projector that will, as the result of an electronically coded message added to the tape cassette, automatically change the slide in line with the taped message. This equipment is also used in the production of the tape to add the electronic signal to the appropriate parts of the tape. More complex presentations of this nature can be produced in multiprojector presentations, controlled in the way just described or, increasingly, by a computer program.

Even more effective for single projector use is a combined tape-slide presenter. This is basically an integrated unit containing a slide projector, an in-built tape recorder and a television-style, back projection screen. The tape will have been electronically coded to change the slides at the appropriate intervals and their images will be projected on to the back projection screen. Most tape-slide presenters nowadays also include a folding mirror which, when raised, can project the image on to a conventional projection screen, the presenter acting more as a normal tape-slide projector combination.

Operation and use is simple, within the constraints already mentioned, requiring the pre-loading of the projector carousel with the slides in the required order and the insertion of the pre-recorded cassette. Focusing of the projected image is frequently an automatic operation of the equipment, and of course the selection and change of slides is automatic.

This operation is usually straightforward, but variations are possible. It is normal to present the slides one after another in a logical sequence. If a change is necessary during the presentation this can often be brought about by the intervention of the trainer, perhaps by means of a remote control. In this way the presentation can be halted and the projector reversed to show an earlier slide. However, the synchronization would then be thrown out of kilter. One way of avoiding this, if the replay of a particular slide may be needed, is to add a second slide of the same subject. Alternatively, it is possible to obtain presenters that include a microprocessor and can be linked to a computer. In such cases it is the signal from the microprocessor or computer program that tells the projector which slide to select and the period of time for which to show it. However, even with this up-to-date technology there is some reduction in flexibility from the manual control of a live trainer/ presenter. The criterion must be whether or not any flexibility is required, or whether the programme can be presented in the same way on every occasion.

These combined presenters are usually problem free, although with both projector and recorder difficulties can arise from time to time, so I would be wary of taking too much account of a recent advertisement that suggested setting up the equipment and leaving it to run itself completely – frequently a recipe for disaster!

Advantages and disadvantages

ADVANTAGES

- A professional-looking presentation
- Uses high quality, colour-impactive slides
- The equipment is reasonably portable
- The slides and cassettes are readily storable and easily portable
- In many cases, *minimal* attendance and control is required

---

DISADVANTAGES

■ Preparation can be extensive and costly
■ Equipment is costly (minimum £700)
■ A darkened room is necessary when used in normal projection mode
■ Slide-tape presenter has a small screen and so is suitable for small groups only
■ Operation wholly dependent on electrical stability and problem-free movements

---

Preparation of tape-slide presentations

Because of the extended complexity, more detailed attention and preparation is required for a tape-slide presentation than for a straightforward input session, whether the tape-slide is used as the session or (even more) as an integrated part of a complex session.

The necessary steps are as follows.

1. Decide whether the tape-slide input is to be the complete session or an integrated part of it.
2. If part of the session, determine the reasons for using a tape-slide insert and the objectives for that part of the session.
3. If this is your normal practice, produce a story-board for the presentation section, for both audio and slides.
4. Produce a script for the audio content, written in the exact format and wording that will be used, annotating the points at which a slide change will be necessary. You will almost certainly need to rehearse this before making a recording. It will also be necessary to include notes on the slide to be used, the length of time needed for the slide to be showing, pauses, breaks, etc.
5. Collect and assemble the relevant slides into the order determined by the audio script, including duplicate slides or blank slides as necessary.
6. Record the audio, producing as clear and high quality a recording as possible within the constraints of the equipment and facilities available to you. It can be helpful to have the slides mounted in a slide projector that has editing capabilities so that you can see the slides as you record.

7. Add the control coding to the sound track for synchronization. This can be performed at the time of the recording but it is usually more effective to concentrate on the recording at first, picking up the coding at greater leisure.

8. Have a dummy-run presentation, varying the audio stage and the control coding if necessary.

9. Produce handouts for the learners, based on the tape-slide presentation.

10. Finally, have a contingency plan in case major problems arise.

VIDEO

The tape-slide presentation is in many respects the half-way house between audio aids and television that combines sound with moving vision, the modern development from the film projector. This latter was a friend to training and development practitioners in the pre-1970s, albeit a variable friend, needing considerable care in setting up and prone to frequent breakdowns. Modern television and allied video techniques, being electronically controlled, are not totally safe from problems, but these are considerably fewer than with the usual film projector used by trainers.

'Video' is a term given to a range of techniques in training and development and it has many uses as a training aid. The principal types are:

- commercially or internally produced video cassettes as the training session
- commercially or internally produced video cassettes as part of the training session
- video recording during the training event by means of closed-circuit television (CCTV) or direct camera work
- interactive video and interactive compact disc (CD-I).

The video as the training session

There is nowadays, because of the increased use of video over audio alone, a large variety of training videos in a wide range of subjects: in fact, from the resources of the combined video producers, it would be difficult not to find a suitable video for every major aspect in the training field. The majority are cassettes with durations of between 20 and 40 minutes, more usually the former. Consequently they are either summaries of or introductions to a subject, or more detailed investigations of small parts of a subject. This has an influence on their use in training and development.

The video cassette is played through a video player – this is the instrument that is commonly referred to as the 'video' – in a similar way to the audio cassette and the audio cassette player/recorder. The images are then transferred to a television monitor, in some cases one which is a television projector without the full facilities of receiving broadcast TV programmes. However, the custom-made monitor is not essential, with video cassettes being playable through ordinary television receivers. This combination is demonstrated in Figure 7.3.

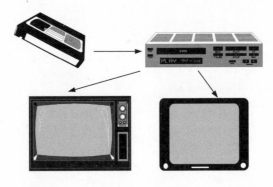

Figure 7.3 *The video playing combination*

The principal problem encountered in using a video with a learning group is that, even with large-size monitors or receivers, the projected image is still quite small and so the video can be used effectively with only a relatively small group if all members are to see the action clearly. One solution for this, particularly with a very large group, is to use the image projection equipment (see Chapter 5). A relatively small image can, with this equipment, be projected on to a very large screen.

Pre-recorded videos used as part of a training session are projected in a similar way.

Video recording during the training event

In this case we are starting with a blank video cassette and producing our own programme for projection in the manner described above. However, additional equipment is required for the earlier part of the process, namely CCTV or a video camera, both linked to the video recorder. CCTV usually means a video camera permanently installed in the 'training' room. In order to make the camera less conspicuous it is usually mounted at about ceiling height, in a corner, and part covered by an opaque covering. Unfortunately this attempt at deception can often have the opposite effect and make the set-up even more obvious. The alternative is to have a video camera mounted on a tripod and placed as unobtrusively as possible in the room – it is still obvious, but because there has been no attempt to hide it its presence can be accepted much more quickly.

In order to intrude on the training event as little as possible the camera movements, focusing and field of view are all controlled by the trainer from a console in another room, the projected images being shown on a monitor. Part of this combination is shown in Figure 7.4.

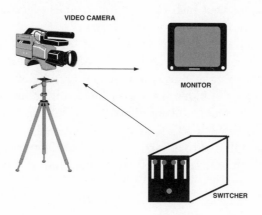

Figure 7.4 *A remotely controlled video camera combination*

PRE-RECORDED VIDEOS

As described above, these videos can be used in two way – as the training session itself or as part of the session. In the latter case part of a full video or specially produced 'trigger' videos can be used.

The video as the training session

The comments about any training aid apply equally to videos – they are aids to training and development and can rarely stand alone. This would seem to be a contradiction when we are considering a 20 to 40 minute video covering some aspect of a training subject. Indeed, in the early days of videos, when they appeared to offer everything the trainer wanted, they were used as substitutes to the training, rather than as supportive aids. A video would be played before a group of learners with no further action at the end – *'The video said everything, so why go over it again?!'* was the frequent comment. This would be acceptable if for every subject there was only one approach, only one answer, or every learner accepted without question the message projected by the video. Fortunately this is not so.

A common, though not necessarily effective use of the video as a training aid is to reduce the expenditure of time and money. A typical scenario in training and development nowadays is for a training video to be the 'main event' in a short (say, one-hour) training session mounted over the lunch period for volunteer learners who are willing to give up their free time for their own development. There are in fact some organizations that insist that training takes place at times such as this; fortunately these are not *too* common.

The traditional approach in an event of this nature would be to introduce the video by stating its title and general nature – eg 'This is a video about coaching' – show the video and, at the end, say in effect 'Well, you've seen the video; now you know all about coaching. Go out and coach.' The real result could not be further from this statement. If the 'learners' have actually watched and listened to the video, this passive attitude will instil perhaps 5 per cent of the message, less than 1 per cent of which will probably be retained. Skills cannot be learned from the passive act of watching a video.

More realistic stages for presentation of the video would be:

STAGES FOR USING A VIDEO
IN TRAINING

- OBTAIN THE VIDEO AND VIEW IT YOURSELF
- BEFORE PRESENTING THE VIDEO, ASK YOURSELF RELEVANT QUESTIONS
- ARRANGE THE VIDEO SHOWING
- INTRODUCE THE VIDEO FULLY
- SHOW THE VIDEO
- AT THE END OF THE VIDEO ENCOURAGE LEARNER REFLECTION
- DISCUSS THE VIDEO MESSAGE
- IMPLEMENTATION OF THE LEARNING

---

1. Obtain the video and view it yourself, if necessary several times, so that you are fully *au fait* with its content and the message it is trying to put across.
2. When deciding to present the video, ask yourself the questions:
   - 'What am I trying to achieve?'
   - 'Will this particular video support me in my attempts to achieve these objectives?' 'Is this video relevant to the subject?' (It is surprising on how many occasions videos are shown, ostensibly for a particular training purpose, but actually because the trainer likes the video, even though it may not be completely relevant!)
   - 'Is this the most effective video available?'
   - 'Will the learning group understand it?'
   - 'To what extent will the group agree or disagree with the message?'
   - 'How will I start a discussion following the video?'
   - 'What do I want to achieve during this discussion?'
   - 'What types of questions should be addressed?'
3. Make the necessary arrangements for the video showing, within any constraints that exist, including appropriate equipment, ensuring that it is in full working order.
4. At the start of the session do more than put the video on 'cold'. Introduce the subject briefly and describe what the video is about; say why you are showing it; and what they should be looking out for. Describe what will happen following the video – completion of a reaction questionnaire; a discussion; completion of an assessment questionnaire; and so on.

   If the video content, although appropriate to the subject being considered, is placed in an environment or culture different from that of the group, comment on this fact, but suggest that the message is common and the group may wish to relate it to their particular situations.
5. Show the video. Stay in the room yourself and demonstrate by your example that the video is worth watching – your disappearance might give the reverse message – and remember Murphy and the possibility of the equipment not behaving as it should. You should stay however many times you have seen the video, and also exhibit interest that you hope will be modelled by the group. They will certainly be aware of your presence and attitude.
6. At the end of the video allow a few moments for the group to return to the real world and start thinking about what they have seen. I have always found it helps the group to collect and rationalize their

thoughts to give them a pre-prepared questionnaire asking relevant questions about the video content and seeking their views on various aspects. The questionnaires can be used by the learners as reminder briefs during the ensuing discussion. It is of no value to ask simply 'What did you think of that?' More often than not this is greeted by the response it deserves – silence. Follow the pattern of the questionnaire, posing the questions that are included and for which the participants have prepared. However, be prepared to be flexible and change the order of the questions or encourage discussion on additional subjects as long as they are still relevant to the video subject.

If the group is prepared and supported in this way the discussion can extend over a long period of time, much longer than the time used by the video itself. Consequently you must control this discussion if time is severely restricted, but remember that the discussion is a very strong learning event itself.

7. The final question should be concerned with how the learners could translate the video's message into real-life action. This period of the discussion should include an attempt to obtain commitment from them to do something back at work, in effect an informal approach to action planning. Implementation methods can be discussed in addition to the involvement of the learners' line managers, staff or colleagues. Where appropriate you should contract to support the learners in this by means of discussion with others and/or further learning approaches.

From the guidelines described above it will be obvious that there is considerably more to using videos than simply showing them.

The video used during a training event

Similar processes to the aforementioned can be followed when the video is used *during* a training event, when the video can be used for a variety of purposes, including:

- providing an introduction to the particular subject
- demonstrating one approach to the activity or problem
- modelling approaches and behaviour in such circumstances
- starting a discussion
- acting as an icebreaker
- acting as a reviver or stimulant when the day is flagging – the change of pace, presenter, technique, etc can help to provide this stimulant

- demonstrating the results of certain actions in the circumstances and providing the opportunity for the group to discuss possible alternative approaches
- providing 'practical' evidence of an environment, culture or action that could not, or would be too dangerous to replicate in the training event
- acting as a summary of the training session overall.

The video in self-instruction resources

Many open learning, distance learning and self-instruction resource packages, in addition to text material will have videos as part of the coordinated learning strategy. It is essential that these resource packs include full and appropriate instructions as to the use of the video, which must be accompanied by associated material and activities as described above, modified for self-learning. It is insufficient to include a direction to 'View video 1 at this stage' without suggesting supporting activities.

The video used as a trigger

Whether you are using the video as a short, stand-alone event, as a singular event within a training course or as part of a self-instruction package it is not always necessary to use the complete video, or use it completely in one viewing. This lesson has taken some time to be learned, probably because we were conditioned to sitting in front of the 'box' at home and watching a complete programme.

In training, however, it is becoming the norm to show only parts of the video at one time, using these as triggers to discussion. Fenman Training were in the van in introducing trigger videos, specially constructed as a series of small cameos which are intended to be interrupted at the end each so that questions such as 'What would you do now in this situation?' or 'How would you deal with this problem?' can be raised. Any video can be used in this way, stopping it when a certain event is about to happen or has just happened, and raising the relevant questions, but customized trigger videos make the process easier.

Using videos as a trigger means that you must be very aware of the video and what it contains, so that you can decide how you are to use it. This is particularly the case if you are going to interrupt a full video, as you must be aware of the signal points prior to the parts at which you intend stopping it. An alternative, although my preference is for full awareness of the development of the video, is to run the video through prior to the event and note the video player counter readings at the significant events. When you are using the video you can then simply watch for your noted counter reading. However, beware of counter readings not always being completely accurate – for example, you have to ensure that you rewind the cassette to the same point on each occasion when you are zeroing the counter.

Some commercially produced videos, although 'full' videos, have been made in such a way that triggering is easy. The view context is normal, but at stages throughout there are summaries of the key subject areas covered to that point or in the latest section. This is an opportunity for the video to be interrupted and a discussion commenced on the basis of the summary shown – which can, if necessary, be held on the screen as a reminder.

Other video have what is basically a continuous play format, but at certain stages interruptions are built in. If, for example, an interaction is taking place between two people, just before one of the participants responds to an action of the other, the video instruction is to stop and the question is posed 'What would you do now?' After the break, the interaction continues with a demonstration of what happened (according to the video producers). You can either continue, accepting with the agreement of the group the video answer, or the tape can again be stopped to discuss this 'right answer'.

CUSTOM-MADE VIDEOS

DO-IT-YOURSELF

Videos need not necessarily be purchased from commercial producers. It is possible to make your own, although the quality may not be up to professional standard.

VIDEO EQUIPMENT

The video camera

Professional producers use high-band, top quality, very expensive equipment with consequent optimum results. If you want to make a video without the quality of the professional, you can do so with more or less standard equipment. You will need a good quality video camera using one of the VHS or other formats.

The current choices are VHS (the standard size video cassette); VHS-C (this uses the small cassette similar to an audio cassette); Super VHS; Hi-8 or Video 8. These formats use 13mm- (½ inch) wide tape, apart from Video 8, which uses 8mm tape.

If you are making temporary recordings in which very high quality is not required, VHS (-C) is quite satisfactory, although if you need to copy and edit the recording the copy from VHS is significantly poorer than the original. VHS-C cassettes can be played back on standard video recorders using a special adaptor.

Super VHS uses high quality tape from which excellent copies can be made, although similarly high quality recording equipment is also necessary.

Many video cameras, certainly 'camcorders', have a built-in recorder; otherwise a camera linked to a video recorder will be necessary.

The video recorder

Unless you are simply transmitting the camera image to a monitor, viewing the live image, you will also need a video recorder. This equipment doubles as a recorder and playback instrument and must be compatible with the tape format in use – Super VHS and Video 8.

Viewing equipment

The transmitted image, whether or not it is to be recorded, can be viewed directly. The alternatives are a standard television receiver tuned (usually) to the VCR channel, or a video monitor. The monitor is used for this purpose only and produces a much sharper and higher quality image than the television receiver as the signal has to pass through fewer stages to produce the image.

Lighting

Production of your own video will require a studio of some kind, the larger the better, although with an appropriate camera lens set a lot can be achieved even in a small space. Unless you are videoing outside – and this can cause lighting problems – you will need suitable lighting arrangements. Many of the lighting 'rules' are taken from still photography so this is not a completely new and strange world.

You will need a minimum of two lights, although third and fourth lights can be useful. One light is the key light that provides the main lighting; another is the fill-in light, used to soften or eliminate shadows. The third is used to exclude unwanted shadows from the background and the fourth for backlighting with special effects.

Diffusers or coloured filters can be used on any of the lights to modify the natural effects, and reflectors (sheets of either paper or metal) can be helpful in certain conditions.

A typical studio lighting set is shown in Figure 7.5.

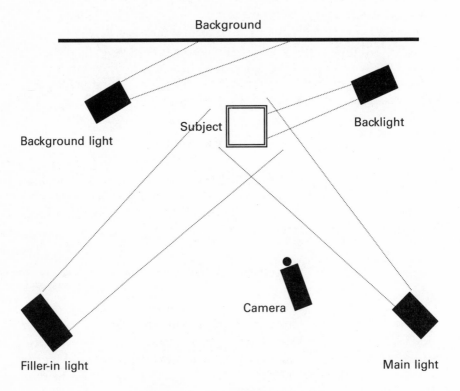

Figure 7.5 *A studio lighting set*

Editing equipment

One of the major differences between the 'home movie' and the 'professional' videos is that the former are usually left as shot, whereas the latter are edited to produce the best final video. To achieve a more professional video some form of editing equipment will be necessary, which is usually quite expensive. The original video tapes are viewed through the equipment and cuts are made or sections are spliced into other parts of the tape. A caveat – it is easy to destroy the original tape in this process, so a copy should always be made.

At this stage various effects can be added – titles, colour effects, graphics as additional frames or superimposed on existing ones, split screens and fades.

Editing is not easy for the inexperienced and the end result (particularly if copying is involved) can suffer from loss of picture quality.

Microphones

The advice given for audio recording is relevant here. Clip-on microphones, either on-line to a mixer or radio versions, stand mikes, hand-held, directional mikes or boom-located ones can all be useful depending on the circumstances.

The actors

Some of the results will be poor – examples can be seen in many home videos – but one essential criterion must be that the quality will not interfere with the learning process. The advantages are that you can customize your video exactly to the environment and culture of the learners. Although the range of commercially produced videos is large, it may be that there is not one exactly suiting your requirements. The 'performers' in the video need not be good actors (although this is to be preferred), but their lack of skill may be offset to some extent by the fact that they may be known to the audience.

COMMERCIALLY PRODUCED VIDEOS

If the money is available professional expertise can be hired or the video production can be contracted out. If this route is followed a comprehensive brief must be produced, and time spent on this will be found to be worthwhile. The production company must be chosen carefully, either through recommendation or by inspecting videos produced for organizations similar to your own. The steps to follow in planning and choosing include:

```
TRAINING OBJECTIVES
TARGET AUDIENCE
STYLE
INVOLVEMENT
COSTING
CHOOSING THE COMPANY
CONTRACTS
```

Training objectives

It should go without saying that the objectives for the video must correlate with those for the training programme in which it will be contained. The first decision will be whether or not a video is the appropriate vehicle for that part of the programme, rather than 'it would be nice to have a video here'! The production company must be made fully aware of both these objectives.

Target audience

This factor must be considered in the same way as when planning a training programme. Questions about size of audience, age, status, understanding level, etc must be asked so that the end product is valid for the audience.

Style

This aspect, which is linked to the story-line, must consider whether the video is to be full-length, a trigger, or an interrupted process with short sequences. Videos can be dramatic, controversial, have right/wrong answer sequences, and so on. You will need to ensure that the producing company has a clear view of what you want.

Involvement

Are you going to leave everything to the producing company, or are you to be involved in some stages or events? Who will select the actors? Can people from your organization be included? Who is to be responsible for ultimate production decisions? Who is to act as liaison adviser? These and other aspects must be clear to you and be made clear to the producer.

Costing

You will have a budget for the video. This will certainly be relevant in selecting the appropriate production company, and the effects that can be included. This cost/inclusion will be relevant in your negotiations with possible producers and you must be prepared to reduce your requirements in view of the cost – but not without strong negotiation.

Choosing the company

Various features affecting this choice have already been mentioned, but try to ensure that your choice is right, since a considerable amount of money can be involved.

Contracts

Many production companies will have standard contracts. Ensure that everything you want is included, otherwise you will need to produce your own. Your legal department must vet this, as contracts can be complex agreements and must be watertight. The contract must include your clear and comprehensive brief to the producer so that there can be no arguments over requirements at a later stage.

VIDEO RECORDING DURING TRAINING

The use of videos in training includes the very common one of recording the course members during the course. These recordings are in the main used for reviewing the activity and aiding the feedback given by other means. High quality equipment is not required in these circumstances, although the better the equipment the more effective will be the recordings, and the more they will help the review and feedback viewings as opposed to trying to interpret fuzzy images. A camcorder as used for home videos will be quite suitable, particularly if the camera is mounted on a tripod. These cameras are much smaller, lighter and more portable than their professional relations.

Virtually any training situation is a suitable subject for video recording, although there are occasions that will be more suitable than others. Here are some examples.

■ Role-plays in a one-to-one situation when the participants are practising interviewing skills. Usually only one camera is used, concentrating on the *interviewer*, but sometimes it is necessary to closely examine the actions and reactions of the person being interviewed. One camera can cover both participants, but depending on the environment, it may be necessary or desirable to use two cameras – remember, however, that the more the equipment the more obvious it is to the learners and the greater the possibility of something going wrong. Two camera and recorder set-ups can be used or, as described earlier when discussing audio recording, a mixer can be used to switch views. This, of course, ties up the trainer or someone else to operate it.

■ Practice negotiations can also be recorded. In this case almost certainly more than one camera with mixing facilities will be needed as both 'sides' are learning the skills of negotiation. Again, however, it is possible to utilize only one camera, using a wider-angle lens to produce a large enough field of view. There may be some lack of clarity, but one camera will always be better than none.

■ Practice, or real, presentations are very suitable subjects for recording in this way and provide the presenters with a permanent record to which they can refer at any time, following their use of the recording as a feedback instrument.

■ You can even record yourself when, for example, you are trying out a new presentation or input session. Viewing the recording will help you identify elements you can modify to improve your performance.

Making a video recording of the activity

This part of the training process should not be approached lightly. Because the medium is so powerful failure can be equally powerful. The stages for setting up for video recording include the following.

1. PREPARE THE EQUIPMENT
2. CHECK POSITIONING
3. CONSIDER USING MORE THAN ONE ROOM
4. PREPARE THE INVOLVED PARTICIPANTS
5. BE AWARE OF DIFFERENT ATTITUDES TO CAMERA PRESENCE
6. BE PREPARED TO IGNORE THE EARLY PART OF THE RECORDING
7. PREPARE THE OBSERVERS FOR THEIR DIFFERENT ROLE

1. **Prepare the equipment**

   Never assume that what has been working well will continue to do so. What worked yesterday may not work today. So, well before the actual event, check that the equipment, having been set up, works properly. It is worth also checking that all connections, plugs, sockets and leads are in order; batteries, when used (and remember if the video recorder is fed by mains electricity that power failures do happen) should be checked for capacity; and microphones and allied equipment should equally be in order. Make very sure that the mounting for the camera, whether on a tripod or other support, is substantial and not in any danger of slipping or being knocked over.

2. **Check positioning**

   Ensure that the camera(s) are in the correct position(s) to record the people and the events clearly and that there is sufficient light. It is advisable not to have the camera pointing in the direction of the strongest light source; if lights are used these should be on each side of and slightly behind the camera, pointing towards the subjects' positions. Check this in the same way that you would for using an OHP or flipchart, but in the reverse direction. It has been mentioned earlier that the camera should be placed in the optimum position to record the activity, but in a position where it will be least conspicuous.

3. **Consider using more than one room**

   If you have more than one room available, and it is possible to run cables between them, it can be helpful to have the camera only in the activity room, and the recorder/mixer/monitor combination in the other. In this way the camera can be less conspicuous and disconcerting to the participants. The camera and its movements can be controlled by a master operator in the other room and the event viewed on a monitor. The remainder of the group acting as observers can watch this monitor, record their observations, and perhaps note significant events on the recorder counter readings. One disadvantage is that if there has to be switching of cameras or focus, etc, this will usually be performed by the trainer, with a consequent diminution of that trainer's observation of the event.

4. **Prepare the participants**

   Role plays and some other activities on a training course can be quite daunting for the learners, and the additional worry of a recording video camera, or the knowledge that others are watching them remotely, may have unfortunate consequences. Some people have an uncontrollable fear of being observed by a camera, others are indifferent to its presence, still others can take an aggressive attitude to being recorded. This should be discussed with the learners before any video recording takes place and, if the 'anti' feeling is very strong, it may be necessary to avoid using it. However, it should be pointed out that by not using it the opportunity for objective review and feedback will be lost to a significant extent. Above all do not make an issue of it – if there are a number of events to be videod the objectors may change their minds when they see the value of the process when their fellows have been through it.

It is often possible to reassure participants who are concerned by (a) advising them that they will forget about the camera after a short period of time, and (b) the recording will only be seen by those whom they agree should view it – usually the learning group or even just the immediate participants.

Often even more difficult to control are the people at the other end of the spectrum – the ones who cannot wait to get in front of the camera to perform! By all means try to reduce this thespian attitude, but do not be too concerned as, when the participants become involved in the activity, they too will forget about the camera and start behaving naturally. You may, however, have to ignore the first five minutes or so of the activity.

5. **Prepare the observers**

    In addition to the participants who are directly involved in the activity, some or all of the remainder can be used as observers whose role it will be to assist in the review and feedback. These too will need to be prepared, in addition to the preparation required for their normal observation roles. This preparation will be concerned with the differences of observing 'remotely', the difficulties of concentrating for periods of time on a small monitor and the need, at the same time, to note the recorder counter readings for the figures at significant events.

Use in review and feedback

The principal use of video during training is as an aid to the review and feedback of the learners' activities, whether in a one-to-one or group situation. Viewing the recording obviates the possibility of disagreement with the feedback – if the recording is clear, the particular point being made should be equally clear.

Review and feedback of performance of participants on training courses is usually by means of the visual observations of the trainers and/or observers taken from the group. At the end of the activity the common approach is to merge comments from the participants with those of the observers and the trainers. Frequently this feedback can take much longer than the activity itself, and there are a number of different methods of practising this review (for full descriptions of various methods see Rae (1996), among others).

Some of the alternative methods for using the recording in the review include the following.

- If video recording is used to observe the activity, the first consideration is that it really *must* be used after the activity in some way, otherwise there is the danger of rejection by the learners, not only of video recording but other training activities. This may appear simple to implement, but there are a number of problems. There can be no doubt that the use of a video recording in review and feedback adds time to this part of the learning process. The recording cannot stand alone as the feedback vehicle; there will always be the need for verbal discussion with all the people involved in the process and the additional video feedback is time consuming.

- The first, apparently obvious method is, whether other verbal feedbacks are used or not, to play the recording through, the participants, observer and trainer stopping the recording at significant points and making feedback comments. This in fact should be the method used as a last resort only, as not only does it take up considerable time, but also the process becomes boring for all concerned.

- The next, more reasonable approach is to use the whole video, but fast forwarding to the recorder counter readings noted by the observers and the trainer at significant points. This is excellent from the point of view of the observers and trainer, but the active participants might wish to refer to other events and this will involve a considerable amount of searching backwards and forwards to find the required point on the tape.

- Similar to the previous method, but taking even more time, is to link verbal feedback from all the participants and observers with reference to the video on a 'hope we can find the place' basis or with restrictions to the noted significant points. Within this method a number of compromises are possible to reduce the time involved and make referencing easier.

- A more acceptable method is to avoid the use of the recording *at the time of the review*. Immediately following the activity a verbal review can be undertaken using the observers, the trainers and the active participants to highlight the feedback elements. If that event was one of a series of similar events, the two active participants (or the presenter if the activity was one of presentation) can be excused participation so that they can go to a separate room to view the recording, bearing in mind the comments made during the verbal review. Remember, however, that there must be some arrangement made for the recording viewers to report back and make some comment on what they have seen in relation to the comments made – this can become quite complicated.

■ If the event had been part of a number taking place simultaneously, each event participant having their own observer or set of observers, this group can be the one excused further activity to view the recording and discuss it in their own sub-group. Obviously much will depend on how the events to be discussed have been arranged.

■ The other major approach to the use of the recording in review is to follow normal verbal review processes – whether full group or 'family' group and reassembled full group – but not to use the video recording at that time. Reference should be made to significant events that will be observable on the video, and the video recording and facilities should be given to the participants to view it during free time. Recordings of presentational skills events can be given to the presenters to take away with them for viewing (at home or work) after the training event.

The above, which are by no means all the possible combinations of video recording and verbal reviews, suggest that there are many ways of using the techniques. Much will depend on the event itself, but remember that their use is not simple, and in almost every case will add time to the review session or the event.

INTERACTIVE VIDEO AND CD-I

These are specially produced videos, and the current development in pre-recorded material is the interactive compact disc (CD-I). Both have particular applications in training, in particular where self-instruction and open learning are involved.

Interactive video

The first named (IV) of these two aids to training has been around for at least 15 years. In its early form it consisted of a large video disc linked to a monitor and a computer program. Since that time the equipment and techniques have progressed through a number of stages and, with laser techniques being employed, are now significantly more compact. The principle behind the technique is that (originally with still scenes but now with moving images) a scenario or set of linked scenarios is presented. At the end of each scenario or other stage the viewer is either asked what they would do or (more usually) given a multiple choice question. To this stage the approach is similar to the interrupted video described earlier, but in this case the viewer then interacts with the program by keying the answer or number that represents their choice. The program then either accepts the answer as 'correct', tells the viewer that another choice would be more appropriate, or that the response is incorrect. The viewer is then either given another opportunity to respond in a more appropriate manner, or is told what the correct answer should have been and the reasons for this.

Interactive video is a useful vehicle for self-instruction, although a number of IV stations can be used in group instruction.

Immediately some problems can be identified.

- Appropriate equipment has to be available – expensive equipment that is normally used by one learner at any one time.
- The program is completely inflexible – the 'correct' response depends on the model followed by the writer of the program. If the task being performed has one answer only – a very rare event apart from procedural tasks – this is no problem, but, particularly in the case of people problems and interactions, the 'correct' response is more a matter of opinion.
- The program is further inflexible in that the response pattern is passive. If the viewers disagree with the 'correct' response they have either to accept this prescription or abort the program.

Of course, there could (should) be a trainer or subject expert available, even close to hand, although the latter reduces the value of the technique as a self-instruction approach. If the IV is part of a self-instruction, open learning package, this expert should be available via the telephone or, increasingly, through the Internet or E-mail.

CD-I

The latest version of interactive video is the CD-I, which replaces earlier, more cumbersome and space-restricted equipment. With the facilities of the compact disc much more and varied material can be included. The CD-I can be played through a computer, requiring an integral CD player, sound facilities and other special facilities. Alternatively, a separate CD-I player can be used, the material being played through the television receiver or monitor. Because of the extensive space on a CD the 'teaching' capability is not restricted to scenarios, but can include questionnaires and video sequences playable in a much higher quality than is usually possible on the standard personal computer. Possibly the most effective facility is that given to the viewer through a remote controller to move quickly backwards and forwards to selected areas. Interactive activities can be included, and bibliographies and substantial portions of text related to the subject. Handouts and notes can be printed out when the computer is used, but in the case of CD-I player programs hard copy material is also supplied.

Although the CD-I is a considerable improvement on the earlier approaches, many people still view it with suspicion because of its restricted flexibility and prescriptive approach to the solution of problems. Substantial disagreement or lack of understanding do not arise too frequently, but when they do the only recourse is to the (usually human) expert, or facilitator.

Advances in video and computer technologies are taking place rapidly, and the next few years will undoubtedly see even more improvements in technological training aids to help self-developing learners; trainers constructing varied, active and personalized pro- grammes; and aids for coaches performing on-the-job training. One indication of change is the trend for video producers to transfer their products to CD-I or Video CD which offer more features, greater flexibility and ease of use.

8

—

Sight and Sound

A variety of other training aids is available, some obvious as aids, some less so, in which the senses of sight and sound combine to produce an effective learning support. These include:

> - THE COMPUTER AS A TRAINING AID –
>   COMPUTER-ASSISTED LEARNING (CAL)
>   COMPUTER-BASED TRAINING (CBT)
> - THE TRAINERS/PRESENTERS THEMSELVES
> - THE OBJECT
> - JOB AIDS
> - LEARNING LOGS

THE COMPUTER

The computer has changed our lives considerably in the past 20 years or so, both at work and at home. It is not surprising, therefore, that the computer features large in the design, production and use of training aids. The computer does not simply stand alone as a training aid, but as we have seen in previous sections can be of immeasurable use in:

- producing OHP transparencies
- linking OHPs with large screen projectors
- linking video presentations with large screen projectors
- programming tape-slide presentations.

THE COMPUTER AS A TRAINING AID

'OHP slide' presentations

Chapters 4 and 5 described in detail the methods for producing transparencies for use on one of the most common and favourite of the training aids, the overhead projector. The variety that the computer can provide was described and how colour could be included on the slides, either by using outline lettering or printing by means of a colour printer.

However, computer-generated slides need not be converted into OHP transparencies and can be accessible for display in full colour on the producing computer (and virtually any other compatible one), with or without magnified enhancement.

When you are designing and producing a series of slides on the computer for showing by the computer (which becomes in effect a self-contained slide projector), these are formed with a consistent background or border, type of formatting – including lettering standardized over the slide series – and use of colour. Much of the graphic clip-art and pictures available for use are in colour, usually capable of being changed according to the preferences of the designer, and even lettering can be produced in different colours. If an OHP slide is produced on a standard laser printer these colours are translated into black, white and different shades of grey, again capable of being manipulated to emphasize particular points. But essentially they are monochromatic. On the computer screen, if the graphic original is coloured, these colours are reproduced reasonably faithfully and, as mentioned above, the colours can be changed as desired.

The slides can be filed in sets on the computer in the order that you wish and used for similar presentations or training programmes in the future.

The advantages of this include:

- the facility for presenting the same series of slides on a number of occasions
- modification of individual slides by editing when data changes or other formats are preferred
- rearrangement of the slides in between presentations
- permanent retention of a specific slide series.

There are, of course, disadvantages – what system does not have them? – and these include:

- restriction during the presentation to the logical order of showing the slides as determined before the event
- constraint to the slide as produced, during the event
- power supply failure
- small computer screen visibility.

The first disadvantage is not total as the programs are usually sufficiently flexible (unless automatic) to return to a previously shown slide, or to skip a slide or two. However, if the presentation is restricted to manual operation to provide for this eventuality, the often valuable automatic facility has been lost.

Nor is the second disadvantage immutable because, if it becomes known during the presentation that part of a slide is incorrect, the slide *could* be edited. This would not normally be done, however, as it interferes with the flow of the session, much more so than a simple pen alteration on an OHP slide.

Unless there is an alternative power supply, or the computer is battery operated, little can be done if the power supply fails. Battery-operated computers are usually laptop ones with a very small screen, hardly usable in a training session or presentation, and transmission to a large screen projector will require mains power.

The last-mentioned disadvantage is no problem if the learning group is small. If the group is large, provided the facility is available, the computer signals can be sent to a large screen projector, described earlier, whether in the training room itself or with the computer in another room.

If the session has been designed so that the trainer is satisfied with the slides and their order, an automatic facility can be included, perhaps linked to an audio output so that the trainer has simply a control role during the presentation.

Additional and useful facilities include:

- *automatic slide timing* with variable times for different slides, a facility that can be overridden by the trainer/presenter
- *slide transitions* with a black image in between slides, the audience's attention being brought back to the speaker
- *slide dissolving* from one to the next, the speed of transition being controllable, and so avoiding the obvious slide change
- *slides that build* word by word, or line by line (the computer slide equivalent of the disclosure method), and so add movement to what is basically a stationary object; the next word or line appears from the top, bottom or sides of the slide and moves into its correct place, often being highlighted or differently coloured

- *hidden slides* that do not automatically display – the decision whether or not to show a slide during a particular presentation is taken prior to the event, depending on such things as time, the type of audience, confidentiality, and so on, all without actually deleting the slide from the series
- *slide branching* to introduce another slide series into the major series if it is decided that this is what is required
- *branching to another application* by switching in another application – for example, a spreadsheet may be introduced as an up-to-date piece of evidence, part of a report might be called up, and so on
- *complete and simple control of the running* (and stopping) of the program and other associated programs by the trainer from the computer keyboard or mouse; with these two facilities complete manual control can be transferred to the trainer.

The programs that produce computer-generated slides offer a variety of builds, frames and backgrounds, the principal caveat being that you must be careful not to reduce the impact of the slide content with an overpowering background. Figures 8.1 to 8.4, albeit reproduced here in monochrome, illustrate some of the variations possible. Figures 8.1 to 8.3 have a background that does not interfere with the text; Figure 8.4 would require white lettering to show against the dark background.

Universal use of the slide program

Normally the slide program produced on the computer from a particular piece of software is restricted either to that computer or to another computer that contains the program, the slide series being transferred by means of a floppy disc on which the series has been saved. If the computer is part of a network within an organization this facility can of course be utilized for showing the series elsewhere. But some programs (for example, Microsoft PowerPoint) include a special facility that enables the slide program to be used on other computers. Not all the original facilities are available through the application in such circumstances, however; for example, branching to another presentation during a series is excluded.

OTHER COMPUTER-ASSISTED LEARNING

The computer has a number of other uses as a training aid, supporting other forms of approaches. If, for example, on an accountancy

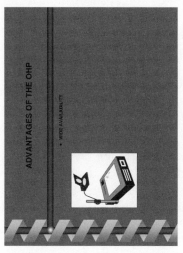

Figure 8.2 *Start of 'build' computer-generated slide*

Figure 8.4 *Example of patterned background for computer-generated slide*

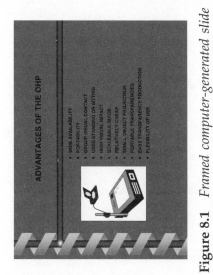

Figure 8.1 *Framed computer-generated slide*

Figure 8.3 *Second stage of 'build' computer-generated slide*

programme the use of spreadsheets is being discussed, the computer is introduced in a natural way as the modern method of producing spreadsheets. A large number of programs are available for the production, completion and maintenance of spreadsheets and these can be demonstrated during the session directly from the computer, using the large screen projector for the group presentation. Computers should be made available for the learners to follow up this input with personal practice.

Similar use of the computer can also be made in respect of learning word processing, program writing, graphs, money programs and so on. When you use the computer in this way as a training aid you should follow, as far as relevant, the general principles of training aids described up to this point. Unless each learner has their own computer or has a networked or slave monitor, and if the large screen projection is not available, the standard computer monitor is suitable only for small groups. Consider carefully the size of, for example, lettering on the monitor for the learners to read and the distance they are from the monitor. As I write this on my computer, I am using Times 12 point lettering, which is quite suitable for reading from the screen (black letters on a white background) at a distance of about 1 metre. Beyond this the clarity and legibility start to reduce. It is possible, of course, to increase the size of the lettering considerably, I use Word 97 as my word-processing program – with this I can place on screen lettering in excess of 1000 point, lettering with a size of about 25cm, although you would rarely want to restrict the content of the screen to this extent.

All the other effects described are available for temporary display – colours, bold lettering, underlining, boxing, bulleting, and so on, and graphics of all sorts. It is obviously advisable, if you are going to use various effects as training aids, that you have these immediately available on a program, although they can be produced in front of the group – this might be an appropriate learning technique in some situations.

COMPUTER-BASED LEARNING (CBT)

If the computer is used as a simple training aid its full capabilities are not being used and an increasing number of situations are becoming suitable for and capable of training through a computer program. Usually this consists of a computer program package, or the package as part of a multimedia one – text, video, questionnaires, projects and activities – relating to a specific subject or range of related subjects. It is almost always used as a self-learning package rather than part of a training event, although most packages can be modified for such use, parts of the package being inserted into parts of the training event.

The advantages of the CBT package include:

> ■ The learners take part in an active form of learning
> ■ Study can be followed at the learners' own pace
> ■ Understanding checks can be built in easily
> ■ The learning can be followed at the learners' place of work or even at home
> ■ Time and resources are used effectively

The accompanying disadvantages are few, and include:

■ this type of learning requires a high motivation and commitment by the learner
■ managerial, trainer or other expert support should be readily available although this is not always possible
■ some isolation may be felt by the learner sitting alone in front of a computer screen
■ some people have an aversion to, or a fear of working with computers, although this is a decreasing problem with their increasing availability and use.

Equipment required

There are two basic requirements:

1. a suitable computer and environment
2. provision of a CBT program.

There is generally a ready availability of suitable computers either at work or at home – obviously the higher the quality and the more facilities the better. With the increase in the availability of programs on CD, with sound and video capability, a multimedia computer is the ideal, one with as high a specification and speed as possible, although slower machines with the required resources will still be suitable as learning aids. At the time of writing (early 1998), typical computers of this nature are Pentium controlled at about 160 to 300 mHz, with sound and a quad- or sixteen-speed, or higher, CD-ROM drive.

Learning packages, usually currently on CD-ROM, are increasingly available in a wider range of subjects from commercial sources at very reasonable cost, particularly when you consider that the package can be used on more than one occasion. It is also possible to get a custom-written program, either within your organization if you have a computer program writer, or from professional houses.

Use of the CBT package is relatively simple once the program has been installed on the computer.

1. The learner is instructed in the operation of the package, although these instructions are frequently an integral and logical part of the program itself.
2. The learners work through the package at their own rate, taking part in the required activities or projects.
3. If difficulties, misunderstandings or non-understandings arise, reference is made to the supporting manager, trainer or other expert, and/or regular interim reviews are arranged. Up until now the normal contact has been in writing or on the phone. With the wider availability of the Internet and allied programmes, greater use is being made of computer-controlled fax contact and E-mail, without the learner leaving the computer.
4. Learning is reviewed and confirmed at the end of the program, with implementation being contracted on an action plan, agreed with the learner's manager, and the learning put into practice.

The use of the computer as a learning aid in training and development is not restricted to running computer programs as just described, or as the means of producing high quality OHP slides or on-computer slides, but in the many linked operations described to this point – interactive video and CD-I, automatic or semi-automatic operation of OHP or other slide presentations, control of other training aid equipment, and so on.

PEOPLE AS TRAINING AIDS

At the other end of the spectrum from complex computers – not even yet the ultimate in electronic wizardry – is the essential human being. Many trainers do not think of people as training aids, particularly themselves, but this aspect can neither be ignored nor left unused. Every time a trainer opens a training programme, whether in front of a group of learners or in a one-to-one coaching or training situation, they are offering themselves as training aids. In the first place, if they were not an aid to the learning by presenting material, activities, etc the learners would be forced to follow the self-learning package route, with limited support in many cases. Second, trainers in the full sight of the learners may, albeit unwittingly, offer themselves as models. When the trainer is presenting an input session how they present, what other aspects they use in the learning programme – discussion, question and answer, activities, etc – and how they respond to and interact with the learners, this presentation has to be as near perfect as possible. There is no place in training and development for the 'Do as I *say*, not as I *do*' attitude – poor techniques are more likely to be challenged nowadays than ignored. Similarly there is no place for a trainer producing a presentation skills programme if they themselves are not good presenters. It surprises many trainers when they receive the comment from learners about why they did something – 'But when you were doing xxx, you did that.'

The trainer as a training aid, in addition to being a suitable model for the learners (and this must be above all the case when trainers are being trained), must also ensure that they are effective training aids in other ways. For example, if questions are asked that cannot be answered by the trainer immediately, the promise is usually made to obtain this information. Failure to do so reduces the credibility of the trainer and also reduces their effectiveness as a training aid.

Near or absolute perfection in the trainer is a lot to ask, but you must be aware of the effects having a considerable impact on the learners. The lead trainer is at the most vulnerable (for obvious reasons) when trainers are being trained and many newly trained trainers have come away from a trainer training programme having modelled themselves on the trainer (for good or ill!). Such role modelling is not to be encouraged, as the learners should develop their own styles, but mimicry is natural, particularly if the trainer is effective (and popular). This singular role modelling can be avoided to some extent in sensitive programmes by using a number of trainers, particularly if they have a variety of styles and approaches. In this way the learners are presented with a number of roles to consider and accept or reject for themselves. This can, of course, have the reverse effect of helping the learners to compare trainers as people in a critical way.

THE OBJECT

Often ignored in the same way as the trainer as a training aid is the object of the training itself. Even small objects that can be readily brought to the training environment are sometimes ignored, the presentation relying instead on photographs, diagrams and other illustrations. If it is physically possible to have an example of the object itself during the learning session, do so – this is the ultimate form of training aid. Rather than have to say 'xxx looks like', you can readily say 'this is xxx'. The use of the video OHP has been described in this context.

The 'object' can be a physical object or an instruction manual, a set of procedures or anything to which direct reference can be made. Its presence brings the subject of the learning to life.

Obviously there will be occasions when it is not possible to bring an object to the training environment, but why not then take the training to the object? If a giant excavator has to be considered, this is obviously too large to bring to the training room. Photographs will help in an appreciation of its features, but even better would be to take the learning group out to a site where the machine is located.

One major advantage of using the object itself as the training aid is that it reduces the amount of verbal description necessary – objects speak for themselves and generally require little or no explanation. In the case of more complex objects, the technique of 'Tell; Show; Do' is a useful training aid – *tell* the learners about the object (its use, history, availability, advantages and disadvantages) as briefly as possible: then *show* the learners the object itself and allow them to inspect it closely, touching, smelling, moving, feeling, etc as appropriate; and finally, if the object is one that works in some way, let them *do* something with it as safe practice before doing it 'for real' back at work.

JOB AIDS

Objects as training aids are often referred to as job aids that can almost stand alone.

Instruction or maintenance manuals

These can be stand-alone aids or ones used in support of other aspects of learning. Care should be taken in assuming that people will learn from even what appears to be a superb manual – this capability is reflected in the person's learning style, discussed at the beginning of this book. Some people can and prefer to learn by themselves, in their own time, in peace and quiet by reading the manual, trying it out, finding problems and solving them by returning to the manual. Others, however, can only learn by listening to somebody describe the operation first, leading them through the steps of learning by practice, then overseeing their attempts at implementation. Yet others learn (albeit not necessarily successfully or in as short a time as desirable) by just trying something out.

Continued development relies in many cases on job aids of this nature – maintenance and repair engineers, for example, constantly refer to their instruction books as they cannot be expected to remember all the aspects of complex items, or recently introduced modifications or new machinery.

Checklists

These can be valuable learning supports, both when learning in the first place to do something that has a set of stages or sequences and later when implementing the learning to ensure that nothing is forgotten. This is particularly true when complex or complicated operations or equipment are involved. Although many people do this unconsciously or subconsciously, for example when starting a car and moving away from the stationary position – this requires only a relatively short mental checklist – other operations, for example preflight aircraft checks, are very extensive, very complicated and it is essential to adhere to sequence and completeness.

Checklists are valuable aids to both the training administration section and the trainer(s) responsible for a training event. Figure 8.5 suggests a checklist that can be used when considering the environment for a training course or major presentation.

Diagrams, charts and posters

If the subject under learning is supported during a programme with a diagram, chart or poster displayed prominently in the training room this aids learning considerably as a constant reminder. The learners have an immediate, simple reference rather than having to ask the trainer, who may not always be available. The learning and its related aid can be continued back at work with the poster displayed in front of the desk, beside the machine, etc. A good example of a training aid of this type is the T-Chart completed by the learners at the start of the

TRAINING ENVIRONMENT CHECKLIST

This checklist is intended as a guide only; omit any items which are not relevant to your actions and add any others that have been omitted.

ENVIRONMENTAL CHECK

Training room(s) booked	...	Syndicate rooms booked	...
Access checked	...	Electrical sockets required	...
Lighting control	...	Ventilation regulation	...
Suitability of rooms	...	Other required rooms available	...
Wall space for posters, etc	...	Posters, screen shots visible	...
Cleanliness	...	Refreshment availability	...
Refreshments ordered	...	Porterage access	...
Parking facilities	...	Sufficient chairs, tables, etc	...
Seating arrangements	...	Toilets locations and availability	...
Telephone access	...	Photocopier availability	...
Fax availability	...	Computer availability	...
Clerical/secretarial contact	...	Directional signs	...

EQUIPMENT

Audio recorder and tapes	...	Video camera, mixer, tapes	...
Video recorder, monitor	...	Extension cords	...
Spare 3-pin plugs	...	Microphones	...
Electrical first aid kit	...	Overhead projector and spare bulb	...
Flipchart and stand	...	Film projector and screen	...
Slide projector and screen	...	Whiteboard and wiper	...
Lectern	...	Computer and peripherals	...
Water carafes and glasses	...	Bottled water, juices, etc	...
Bowls of sweets, etc	...		

MATERIALS

Name tags	...	Blotter pads	...
Small felt tip pens or similar	...	Large felt tip pens or similar	...
Drymarker pens – various sizes	...	Lumocolor pens – water/spirit based	...
Highlighter pens	...	Acetate sheets and rolls	...
Pencils	...	Masking tape	...
Blutack	...	Paperclips	...
Scissors	...	Stapler and staples	...
Hole punch	...	Flipchart paper	...
A4 lined/unlined paper	...	File folders	...
Clipboards	...	Reference books	...
Visual aids	...		

IMMEDIATELY BEFORE EVENT

Check all seating, tables, and extra seating availability ...
Check all rooms available and laid out suitably ...
Check equipment available and working ...
Check refreshments timing, etc ...
Own brief and other resources available and in order ...
Copies and spare copies of handouts available ...
Confirm event attendees' list ...
Confirm guests' availability ...
Secretarial assistance available ...
Clock available, working and correct ...

Figure 8.5 *Training environment checklist*

training programme, showing their objectives, fears, concerns and so on. It is posted to the training room wall for the duration of the event, and referred to at the end of the event.

Other aids

The list of possible job aids is almost endless, being limited by creativity alone. Colour coding in instruction sheets enhances the instructions by concentrating attention on particular aspects. Computer training and further development can be helped by the use of keyboard overlays that summarize the use of the various keys with particular programs. Flashcards, used extensively in education, have a similar role in adult learning – I can recall many years ago having been helped to learn the Morse code by the instructor holding up large cards on which were printed the dots and dashes, requiring immediate response from the group of the appropriate letter.

The job aid can be written (checklists); illustrated (flashcards); or on computer – many programs have help areas, tips that flash on screen during operations or before the start of an application.

Whichever aid is used, general guidelines should be followed:

- DON'T OVERCROWD THE AID
- USE ILLUSTRATIONS AS MUCH AS POSSIBLE
- KEEP THE AID SIMPLE
- ENSURE THAT IT IS COMPLETELY ACCURATE
- TRY TO MAKE IT INTERESTING AS WELL AS INFORMATIVE
- ABOVE ALL IT MUST BE PRACTICAL AND PRACTICABLE

LEARNING LOGS

The Learning Log is primarily a training aid instrument in which learners record during the learning programme events that have become a significant part of their personal learning and which they want to be sure of recalling. This and subsequent use of the logs make them a powerful training aid. Basically they are a development from the informal sheets of paper used by learners on which they made notes as a training event progressed. The log formalizes this action, but extends it by requiring its further use.

The log consists of an introductory, explanatory page followed by a number of sheets in sets of three, one set for each day of the training event. Set-sheet 1 can be used by the learner instead of or in addition to any note sheets that might be made during the training day of interesting, useful or significant learning points. Set-sheet 2 is used by the learners to sort and summarize the points from sheet 1 that they particularly want to recall, perhaps adding references to handouts and other information. Set-sheet 3 is a mini-action plan, detailing from sheet 2 entries that the learner particularly intends to implement and how, etc this action will be taken. The various sheet 3s can eventually be used in the formulation of the final action plan.

The learners usually complete the second and third sheets during the evenings of the course. This gives the them the opportunity to reflect on the day's learning and what it means to them. This reflection and recording supports consolidation and recall of the learning points.

As a further support it is useful to use the first 45 minutes or so at the start of the next training day for the learners to give a short presentation based on their previous evening's log entries. The learners find that in addition to consolidating their learning they are reminded of other learning points by hearing the presentations of their colleagues.

The format of the morning review of the log will depend on several factors – time available, the number of learners, the number of trainers and the type of training event.

If a training group consists of, say 12 learners, the group can be subdivided into two sub-groups that will meet separately and concurrently. If two trainers are available a trainer who would support and guide the presentations can supervise each sub-group. However, if only one trainer is available, the support may be limited to a peripatetic presence by the trainer with each group. At the end of the meetings, the sub-groups could be brought together in the full group to identify and discuss significant issues. As an alternative, albeit one that requires more time and stronger control by the single trainer, is to have the presentations in one large group. The time can be reduced by encouraging the learners to comment briefly on their entries, extending only those that have not been mentioned up to that point. This approach is not as valuable or as satisfying as the small group approach, but it is better than no review at all if circumstances restrict the activity.

Use of the pattern of log completion and implementation should be encouraged to continue beyond the training course, and certainly during the learners' development period and beyond, whenever learning takes place.

Figure 8.6 illustrates an exemplar Learning Log, set-sheets 1, 2 and 3 being shown in an abbreviated form with the sheet titles only. A log would normally be contained in a ring-binder with the introductory pages, and the log sheets, in sets of three, sufficient for each day of the course. Subsequent pages can be added for post-training event use.

AN ALTERNATIVE LEARNING LOG

Many trainers have encountered learners who do not see a particular aid to learning as ideal as they do. This is usually because the aid is too complex, too long or too boring. The training adage KISS – Keep It Short and Simple – should be applied if this is the case because, although the Learning Log is an ideal aid to learning, if the learners do not use it, it is failing in its purpose.

If the Learning Log described above does not appear, Figure 8.7 shows an alternative log that the learners may be more willing to use.

This log would be used in the same way as the one already described, ie completed by the learners during and at the end of the training day, then discussed in small groups the following morning. Completion on a continuing basis after the training programme should also be encouraged.

ANOTHER ALTERNATIVE LEARNING LOG

Learning Logs can take a variety of forms – two have been described and there are several more. Of these others, one of the best is a commercially published log (Honey, 1994). This example is prefaced by an appropriate quote from Aldous Huxley:

> Experience is not what happens to a man; it is what a man does with what happens to him.

This, of course is the fundamental spirit of continuous learning and development, since without it we would be seriously handicapped – never acquiring any knowledge or skills, making the same mistakes repeatedly, and being incapable of adapting to change.

Honey's log consists of a booklet with a number of pre-printed pages with three log sections based on the Learning Preferences – reflecting, concluding and then planning. These will obviously be followed by the 'doing' process. The format of each log sheet is as shown in Figure 8.8.

A LEARNING LOG BOOK

KEEPING A LEARNING LOG

The objective of attending a learning event is to learn something you can use. A complex event can contain a number of ideas, concepts, activities, etc that you might wish to implement at work. It can be difficult, particularly over an extended period, to remember all that you considered, perhaps even some important points.

A Learning Log:

- gives you a permanent document in which to record these ideas as they occur
- helps you at a later stage think about what you have experienced and learned, particularly the key ideas you want to retain
- helps you consider at leisure which aspects you want to implement and how you are going to do this
- is a reminder for you about your intentions when you get back to work
- is a permanent record of your progress and development and of what you have learned.

If the other notes you may have taken and the handouts issued during the training programme are combined with this log, you have a full record of your training to which you can refer at any time.

Your Learning Log should be completed frequently during the event – preferably during periods which may be allocated for this purpose – or during the evening following the training day. Do not leave its completion any longer than this, otherwise there is the danger that some useful and/or important ideas or learning may be lost.

From the first section, review your notes and select the ideas, techniques, suggestions, activities that you feel could be important or significant for you.

In the second section of the log, describe these selections in as much detail as necessary so that you will be able to recall them later.

In the third section, preferably with a priority listing, describe, from your list in the second section, what you are going to implement or otherwise take action on.

- *What* are you going to do?
- *How* are you going to implement or action it?
- *When and/or by when* are you going to implement it?
- *What* resources will you need?
- *Who* can or needs to be involved?
- *What* implications are there for effects on others?

Page 1

THE CONTINUED USE OF THE LEARNING LOG

On the training programme

At the start of the day following the one for which you have completed your log you will, in a small group, be asked to describe the entries you have made. This presentation will:

(a)   help you clarify your thoughts on the area presented
(b)   help you in the recall process
(c)   widen the views of the remainder of the group who may not have seen the implications of the areas you have highlighted
(d)   raise the opportunity for clarification.

As a continuous process

A Learning Log is not intended for use only on training programmes. We are learning all the time, in every type of situation, and a log can help us capitalize on these opportunities. If you read a book and there are ideas that you want to remember and implement, enter these in the log. If, in discussion with others, ideas are suggested that you feel may be of use to you, remember them and enter them in your log at the first opportunity. Keep referring to your log constantly to remind you of activities that you have not yet implemented.

Your line manager in his or her process of your continuing assessment will not only find your log entries valuable in assessing your development, but could be impressed by your intent and persistence.

Remember that if eventually you decide to seek award of a National Vocational Qualification this record can form a useful part of the portfolio you will need to produce.

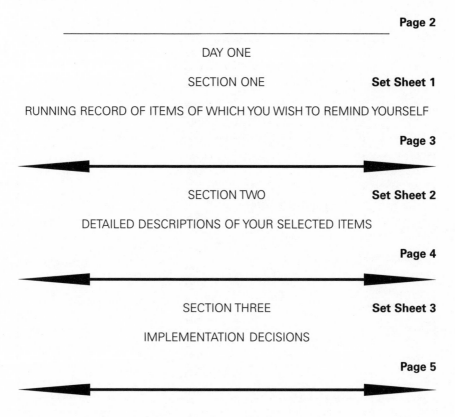

Page 2

DAY ONE

SECTION ONE   **Set Sheet 1**

RUNNING RECORD OF ITEMS OF WHICH YOU WISH TO REMIND YOURSELF

Page 3

SECTION TWO   **Set Sheet 2**

DETAILED DESCRIPTIONS OF YOUR SELECTED ITEMS

Page 4

SECTION THREE   **Set Sheet 3**

IMPLEMENTATION DECISIONS

Page 5

Figure 8.6   *A Learning Log*

LEARNING LOG

Course .... Date ....

Things I want to discuss

Things I want to know more about

Things I want to remember

Things to do

Figure 8.7 *An alternative Learning Log*

LEARNING LOG

Event.. Date ....

My description of what happened

My conclusions/'lessons learned'

My plan to do something better/different

Figure 8.8 *Another alternative Learning Log*

9
—
Handouts

Handouts are part of course documentation or training material and are not normally thought of when training aids are being considered, but they are probably one of the most common aids. We saw earlier that two of the problems of learning are retention and recall. If handouts can be produced so that the learner uses them as references on a continuous and frequent basis, these problems will be lessened.

USING HANDOUTS

Handouts as training aids have a number of uses; formats, times and methods of use vary considerably. Uses include:

- BEFORE THE EVENT AS PREPARATION AIDS
- DURING THE EVENT AS A PREPARATION SUPPORT FOR THE SESSION
- DURING THE EVENT TO SUMMARIZE THE TRAINING TO THAT POINT
- DURING THE EVENT AS AN INTERACTIVE INSTRUMENT
- BRIEFING NOTES FOR ACTIVITIES
- SELF-ASSESSMENT RESOURCES
- LEARNING LOGS
- POST-EVENT REMINDERS

BEFORE THE EVENT AS PREPARATION AIDS

Some form of event documentation can be issued before the event, not to replace it but to prepare the learners for the more detailed or in-depth live sessions. The handout can summarize the areas of learning, recommend pre-event reading and perhaps ask them to carry out some exercises or projects before the event. These might include identifying specific services and practices in their organizations; keeping a time diary; obtaining the views of managers in the organization. A major purpose of the pre-event material is to try to ensure that all the participants will be starting the training at more or less the same level of knowledge. This obviously makes the learning process easier for both the trainers and the learners.

You must not, however, make assumptions about this pre-event handout. First, there is no guarantee that everybody will read it or act on it: in fact, you can be almost certain that somebody will arrive for the event having taken no action at all. This may, of course, not be their fault: they may be a late addition to the course or they may have been forgotten. However, if there are no reasons for learners' failure to read and/or act, you may have problems. Four specific actions for you to take as a result are suggested:

1. Accept the failure and adjust your programme to accommodate the ones who did nothing – if the pre-reading was essential, you may not be able to avoid this.
2. Ignore the fact that essential reading has not been done by one or more participants and carry on as if there was no problem – because of the time allowed for the training you may be forced into this position in spite of the learning problems this may produce.
3. Send the non-performers to a separate part of the training location to catch up with the necessary learning – or as far as is possible at that stage. (This may cause further problems when they return to the event, which will have been progressing in their absence.)
4. A draconian action, but practised by at least one organization of which I am aware, is to send the non-compliers (if the failure could have been avoided) back to their organization. If the pre-work is absolutely essential to the effectiveness of the learning – the event may be very constrained and need to start from a particular point – have you any real alternative?

Of course, the logical way of solving this problem is to avoid it altogether (easier said than done). If the training department link with the learners' line management is good the latter can be brought into the process to ensure that *their* staff complete the essential action for the training they are to attend with *their (the line managers')* agreement.

It can be suggested that, if there are so many potential problems, why invite them by sending out pre-event material? Unless it is completely new material for the learners (when they would be expected all to be at the same zero level) most courses, unless there has been some pre-selection, will start with participants at different levels of knowledge and skills. This does not make the task of training and learning any easier, and has been the cause of many of the bad evaluations of training programmes – not necessarily due to the trainers or the training.

The practical dangers of pre-event reading material

One common problem experienced when the learners have read the pre-event handouts is that they then can attend the event with undesirable attitudes. These can include:

- 'I know all about the subject now, so why should I come on this course?!'
- The learner reads the material again while the course is proceeding, checking that the trainer is in fact saying what is reflected in the handout. A resulting caveat for presenters must be that what they intend to say should not conflict with what they actually say.

DURING THE EVENT AS A PREPARATION SUPPORT FOR THE SESSION

Some trainers prefer to issue handouts related to their session(s) at the start of the session on the basis that this will let the learners know what the session is about and what they should be looking for. This handout can be brief or extended. If it is extensive there are the dangers that it will not be used by the learners or, worse, will be read as the session progresses, the learners, as suggested above, either checking on the trainer or not listening to the presentation.

A much more effective approach is to make this handout very brief, stating only the headlines of the subjects that will be covered during the session, supporting the verbal, summary statement with which the trainer will (should) start the session. Again ensure that there is no conflict between intention and act. However, even this minimal approach distracts the full attention of the learners from what is happening and its use is not really recommended.

DURING THE EVENT TO SUMMARIZE THE TRAINING TO THAT POINT

One of the principal problems with handouts is ensuring that they are read, which is essential if they are to act as a supportive training aid for the session or event. A successful approach to this problem (although it will eat into the practical time of the event) is to issue the relevant handout at the end of a session *and give the learners time to read it*. This latter part is an essential activity and can, if time allows, be developed by discussion or questions on the handout, activity that really should have occurred during the session. You should, however, always welcome questions of clarification, thus ensuring a higher level of learning.

As with all handouts, and perhaps even more so in this case, you should ensure that the handout material accurately reflects the content of the session. There is no argument against including *more* than is mentioned in the session, but you must ensure that the learner is made aware of this.

DURING THE EVENT AS AN INTERACTIVE INSTRUMENT

Questions and answers as a result of the handout issue are included here. The more interactive use of a handout during the event, the less passive the session. Another example might be at the end of a section of the session (or at the end of the session) when a handout is issued which would ask the learners to *do* something, even if this is merely reflecting on what has happened. For example, the learners can be asked to consider what happened in an activity in terms of adding their comments to part narratives about the activity or, even better, have them answer questions about the process and task. Questions might include the following.

■ What happened from their point of view during the activity?
■ What activities contributed to this?
■ Who was involved significantly during the process?
■ What have they learned from the experience?
■ How might they implement the information?
■ What problems might arise from the suggested actions?

A final part of such an interactive handout might be combined with a summary of the learning points, the key areas covered, ideas for implementation and so on, this part of the handout to be read after the interactive part.

DURING THE EVENT AS BRIEFING NOTES FOR ACTIVITIES

These are probably the handouts with the greatest use during a session, being instructions that the learners should follow when they are asked to take part in some form of activity, whether this is a sub-group activity, a singular event or a one-to-one interaction. This handout should supplement the verbal instructions you will be giving before handing out the document, which will describe:

- What the activity is
- What is required as a result of the activity
- How long the learners have to complete it
- How they will be required to report their results
- Any comments about equipment or other resources

There are some general rules about what to include in a handout and how to include it – these will be discussed later – but suffice it to say at this stage that the handout should contain sufficient material to enable the learners to carry out the activity. It should not be so long as to be too complex to be read and understood. This latter point, however, will have to be considered, as the purpose of the activity may indeed be to test the acuity of the learners. Keep the handout brief, with short but understandable sentences; use plenty of 'white space'; and use bullet points and other typographical methods as suggested earlier for visual aids. If at all possible, but not at the expense of clarity, keep the brief on one side of a sheet of A4 paper – if you fill this, redraft the brief as, in many cases, it will be too long.

Above all, give the participants and observers (who will have their own documents as well as observation instruments with which to familarize themselves), sufficient time to read the brief, understand it and remember the key points. Check this almost to the point of annoyance, because on so many occasions groups of learners have blamed the cause of their 'failure' in the activity on having insufficient time to read and learn the brief.

SELF-ASSESSMENT RESOURCES

One of the common handouts used during a session is a request for the learners to complete a self-assessment questionnaire that can then be used during the remainder of the session. A typical example of this is found in interactive or communication training courses. This is the Learning Style Questionnaire (LSQ) used with the learning styles of Honey and Mumford (1982). A common approach is:

- the session starts with a general discussion of the Learning Cycle and the need for learners to follow this effectively
- the LSQ self-assessment questionnaire is then completed and scored
- the results are identified and 'interpreted' in company with a description of the different styles of learning that different people utilize
- the session is then usually completed with a discussion of what needs to be done, what can be done to modify what has been identified and contracting to do it.

LEARNING LOGS

These have been described earlier and are becoming a more common and powerful documentary training aid for the learner, not only during the training programme, but as an instrument of continuing development. After all training and learning does not stop at the end of a training event, of whatever nature, and learning must be considered as lasting for the rest of your life. There appears to be strong medical evidence that when we stop learning the advance of senility increases in pace because we have stopped wanting to learn and be active, at least mentally.

POST-EVENT REMINDERS

These are the documents issued either at the end of each session or at the end of a course, with the intention that they are taken away by the participants as post-event references and recall supports. The obvious hope is that the learners will actually use these, reading and re-reading them and perhaps using them in their implementation of the learning. However, these hopes are not always (often?) fulfilled and their use varies considerably. Typical comments by learners about their non-use of handouts post event range from:

- 'I threw them away before I even left the training room'
- 'When I got back to work, I put them in a drawer and never looked at them again'

through

- 'I look at them occasionally to remind me of the content of the presentation'

to

- 'I frequently refer to them to remind me of the material and motivate me to practise the learning'
- 'I refer to them when I am constructing a presentation/negotiation, etc of my own'
- 'I use them as handouts at my own events!'.

There are obviously pertinent reasons in most cases why the first two comments are made (so frequently). These can range from participants' thinking the handouts badly written to considering that they contain irrelevant or incorrect material. But the principal reason is that they are usually written in a format that does not invite reading. If you write the handout on one side of one sheet of A4 there is a strong likelihood that the handout will be glanced at; beyond that size the likelihood decreases in proportion with the extra sheets!

GUIDELINES FOR WRITING HANDOUTS

Although these guidelines do not guarantee that your handouts will be read or used, they may increase that likelihood.

> ■ Use one side of one sheet of A4
> ■ Re-read and edit it severely
> ■ Is another format more effective?
> ■ Use plenty of 'white space'
> ■ Use copied OHP slides
> ■ Use bullet lists
> ■ Use a variety of typo forms
> ■ Let the learners know whether there will be a handout
> ■ Wherever possible use graphics

- Use one side of one sheet of A4 paper wherever possible. The sight of several sheets of text tends to make many people shy away from reading any of them. One sheet does not seem as daunting.
- If you have to use more than one sheet, re-read what you have written and edit it severely – you may in fact be able to reduce it considerably yet still leave a sensible and usable document.
- If in the end you have to use more than one sheet, consider whether there is another format in which it can be produced, eg as key words or phrases rather than continuous text – remember the advice given for constructing visual aids. You can allow yourself a little more licence, but keep it under control.
- Use plenty of 'white space' for ease of reading and impact. Uncrowded pages are easier to read and encourage the learner to do so. Figures 9.1 and 9.2 demonstrate the differences between a 'normal' and a 'white space' approach. Figure 9.2 does not go into the same amount of detail as does 9.1, but with the learners having attended a session on this subject all that should be necessary is an impactive reminder of the key points. Which do you prefer?
- Use copied OHP slides. OHP slides you have used as visual aids during the session should be impactive, key point summaries of the various points made. As the learners have seen the slides, a copy of the slide as a handout will help them recall the actual slide and aid retention of the points.
- Use bullet lists rather than text paragraphs – bullets make the entries and the divisions between list items, sections and so on stand out; lists reduce the number of words and make reference easier.
- If they will introduce a higher degree of impact use underlining, boxes, bold and italic lettering, varied lettering fonts, etc, but do not overdo these.

COMMUNICATION SKILLS PROGRAMME

SENSORY LEARNING

Sensory learning includes four preferences that rely on the **sense of sight**:

- *Learning by reading.* This learning preference can be translated into reading information, skill techniques or procedural written material. It is an approach that can be difficult for many and is fraught with problems caused by the level of intellect, understanding capabilities and other considerations such as language.
- *Learning by seeing.* Many people have to see something before they can understand and, as a result, learn. The sight might be the object itself, a model, or even a graphic visual aid or computer graphic.
- *Learning by visualization.* This is a difficult approach that requires the learners, from verbal or written descriptions, to visualize an object, event or concept.
- *Learning by writing.* Whether it is the act of copying something from an existing text; interpreting, analysing and summarizing an extended text; or making notes from a verbal presentation, many people find the act of writing it down helps their learning, retention and recall.

The sense of hearing can have a significant effect on learning by:

- *Learning by listening.* Those who find it difficult to learn via the written word, whether it is through difficulties of understanding or an inherent problem with that medium, will frequently understand and learn from the spoken word.

Figure 9.1 *Part of a 'normal' text format handout*

COMMUNICATION SKILLS PROGRAMME

SENSORY LEARNING

Five senses are used in various forms of learning:

The sense of sight:

The ideal learning environment must be one in which the training makes use of as many of the sensory tools that are relevant and available.

Learning by reading

Learning by seeing

Learning by visualization

Learning by writing

The sense of hearing:

Learning by listening

Figure 9.2 *Part of a 'white space' text format handout*

- Make sure that at the start of the session the learners know whether or not there will be a handout and in what format – for example, a reproduction of an OHP slide used during the session. If there is not going to be a handout, without telling the learners you will be criticized by those who would have taken notes: if there is going to be a handout, without telling them you will be criticized by those who have taken notes but would otherwise not have done so!
- Wherever possible use graphics rather than words, or graphics supporting and giving impact to words. Obviously the graphics must be relevant and easily understandable.

Colour and tinting

Most of your handouts and other written material that are produced 'in-house' will be in monochrome, rather than those from professional printing houses where colours (at a cost) can be included. However, colour shades can be indicated in monochrome by using a percentage of the shades of black. Most computer programs contain a grey-scale line colour and style and a fill range of shading. This commonly runs from solid black (100 per cent), through varying percentages that appear as progressive depths of grey, to clear (0 per cent). These shade fills can be used to modify images, photographs and drawings. Other effects such as 3-D and shadows can vary a straightforward image from monotonous black and white. Figure 9.3 demonstrates a block range of grey-scale shades, and Figure 9.4 some 3-D and shadow effects.

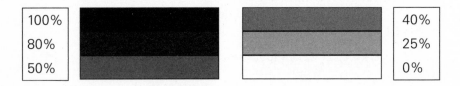

Figure 9.3 *Grey-scale shadings*

Paper

The paper you use for your handouts or other written material offers a significant range of choices, including:

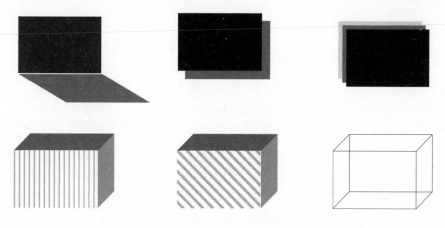

Figure 9.4 *Shadow and 3-D effects*

- COLOUR
- GRAIN
- SIZE
- PAPER:
   TYPES
   WEIGHT

Colour. A wide variety and range of colours and shades are available and can be very useful in providing an immediate identification code. For example, handouts can be printed on white paper, activity briefs on yellow, and so on. Be careful, however, as an indiscriminate use of lots of colours can annoy.

Grain. This may not have too much impact on emphasis or appearance, but some papers benefit from an obvious grain running vertically, horizontally or diagonally, and some have a better appearance without any obvious grain. Heavily grained paper can have an effect on the printing quality and it is certainly more difficult to write with a pen on this type of paper.

Size. Although A4 and A5 are the most commonly used paper sizes, there is a range from large to small, each having a relevance for particular purposes. Paper sizes are described under ISO (International Standards Organization) with A0 as the largest trimmed sheet size of one square metre. The sizes reduce, by halving the preceding size, to A10, which is 26 × 37 mm, intermediate sizes including A4 (half of A3) at 210 × 297 mm and A5 (half of A4) at 148 × 210 mm. A4 is the most commonly used size for handouts since a substantial amount of text and graphics can be included on one page, and it is a suitable size to be fitted into a ring-binder.

Paper types. There are many types of paper, some of the names given being unique to the manufacturer, although common ones are 'cartridge' which is a heavy and tough paper that is almost card; 'bond' a crisp, tough paper with a matt surface; 'wove' a smooth, usually brilliant white with a slightly glossy surface; and 'art' which is very smooth and glossy.

Weight. This factor determines the 'thickness' of the paper and is measured in grammes per square metre and shown by the abbreviation 'gsm' or 'g/m²'. The minimum weight generally used is 90 gsm, which is the lowest weight of paper that can be printed on both sides without the printing showing through – although the type of paper can also affect this. If you want to print on both sides, your safest weight is 100 gsm.

HANDOUT STYLE

This subject can be one of the most controversial in the area of guidelines for handouts. The 'normal' v 'white space' format has been mentioned above and is but one of the areas of possible controversy, the former usually being favoured by people who are not confident that their session was sufficient to enable learning. But other issues can be equally controversial and in many cases evolve into purely personal preference – but is it *your* preference or that of the *learners*?

Consistency

Two principal schools of thought exist in relation to the consistency of handouts – as indeed in many other forms of training aid. Probably the major supporters of the consistency party are book publishers who, in general demand that like items are treated in a similar manner. They disapprove to a large extent of the mixing of typefaces; size of illustrations; and the like, whereas the other camp considers that variety makes for a greater degree of interest and impact. Perhaps in the former's case there is pressure for conformity because of printing costs and the more extensive skill needed by typesetters. In many cases a compromise is not only necessary, but also possible.

Consistency is almost certainly required within one document – I do not mean by this that there can be no mixing at all, but you should make consistent such aspects that, if mixed, would confuse. If, for example, you always use ■ bullets for major items and ● bullets for sub-items, do so throughout the document. It can be confusing to the reader if your stage lists are numbered (1), (2), etc in one part, and (a), (b), etc in other parts. This does not, however, necessarily mean that the next document has to follow slavishly the conventions you have formulated for the first: a change of appearance can often improve impact, leading the reader away from 'Oh, here's the same sort of boring handout'.

If you are going to use personalized or rare symbols, etc in a range of documents, it can be helpful to the readers if you include somewhere, perhaps in a first brief handout, an explanation of what these deviations from the norm are.

Use abbreviations sparingly: you may know what they are, but not every reader will. A useful technique is to spell out in full the word or phrase the first time it is used. After this, the convention is to include the abbreviation in brackets – eg National Vocational Qualification (NVQ) – and I have always found, as a reader, that it is helpful if the abbreviation is then used throughout. However, if the abbreviation is not used regularly, later occasions benefit from a repeat of the full phrase.

Be careful of your grammar and spelling; be consistent. For example, if using 'z' rather than 's' in certain words – organization, formalize, etc – use the 'z' consistently.

But in your handouts do not slavishly follow all the rules, particularly the pedantic ones. Rather ensure that what you are writing is clear, understandable and has impact, while obviously trying to make it as grammatically correct as possible. More detailed comments on grammar will be found on page 170.

The Fog Index

A reasonably objective test to assess your writing is the *Fog Index*, used in sections of continuous text. The Fog Index is calculated as follows.

1. Choose a typical sample of the text.
2. Count to the end of the sentence (to a full stop, colon or semi-colon) taking you past 100 words.
3. Within this total number of words, count the number of sentences.

4. Divide the number of words by the number of sentences = average sentence length.
    Eg 107 words within four sentences = 26.75.
5. In the same sample, count the number of words with three or more syllables (exclude verbs that are made into three-syllable words by the endings '-ed', '-ing' or '-es').
6. Divide the number of 'hard' words so counted by the total number of words and multiply by 100.
    Eg 11 words with three syllables or more in 107 words: $11/107 \times 100 = 10.28$.
7. Add the average sentence length to the syllable product and multiply by 0.4.
    Eg $26.75 + 10.28 = 37.13 \times 0.4 = 14.85$. This is the Fog Index.

The Fog Index runs within a range of 6 to 16 and the originator of the calculation (Gunning, 1952) viewed an Index of 12 or more as text that may be too difficult to read. This Index was constructed originally for US American grade school level, but it gives an *indication* of the writing style.

The Flesch Index

A test that was designed for adults is the *Flesch Index*, a rather more complex approach (Flesch, 1949). In this Index, the steps are as follows.

1. Calculate the average sentence length as in the Fog Index.
    Eg 26.75.
2. Multiply the result by 1.015.
    Eg $26.75 \times 1.015 = 27.15$.
3. Subtract the result from $206.8 - 'x'$.
    Eg $206.8 - 27.15 = 179.65$.
4. Calculate the number of syllables per 100 words.
    Eg 187 syllables.
5. Multiply the result by $0.846 - 'y'$.
    Eg $187 \times 0.846 = 158.20$.
6. Subtract y from x = Flesch Index.
    Eg $179.65 - 158.20 = 21.45$.

The Flesch scale runs from 0 to 100, the lower the figure the more difficult the readability, with the average point being around 64.

Although these scales appear to be highly objective and quantitative, with their arithmetical approach, they should be taken as indications only, as readability will depend on a number of factors.

Lettering, typefaces and points

This subject was discussed when the construction of flipcharts and OHP slides was being considered, with no prescriptive approach being made, but personal preferences (your own and the learners') within reasonable bounds. The same applies to lettering, typeface and size of lettering used in handouts, perhaps even more so as the handout is with the learner longer than the OHP slide.

Again there are no rules set in concrete, except the general approach that the simpler styles are usually the more effective. However, decorative styles and fonts do have a place in a well-designed document.

You will recall the OHP slide discussion of serif v sans serif type and the general conclusion that they can be mixed, but in a controlled manner, one type being used for headings and impact text, and the other for the remainder. At the risk of contradicting what was said under consistency above, it can be helpful to have the main title of the set of handouts in one style, with the rest of the text in a different one. This might be a plain or decorative font. Figure 9.5 compares a small representative selection of some of the fonts available on many computers and software, and demonstrates some of the popular point sizes in use.

Page format

In order to make the document as clear as possible you will no doubt use sentences, paragraphs and sections. The grammatical construction of sentences is simple – they start with an upper case or capital letter and end with either a full stop (.), a question mark (?) or an exclamation mark (!) in ordinary construction.

A paragraph is a sentence or set of sentences, all concerned with related matter and isolated to show this related set separately from other sets. The division of text into paragraphs breaks up what would otherwise appear to be monotonous, continuous text.

The start of paragraphs can be indicated in a number of ways. The straightforward approach is to leave a line space then start at the margin.

This is what this paragraph start looks like, with a line space left after the preceding line.

Otherwise, as with the start of this paragraph, and the ones used generally in this book, the paragraph line after the first (in which the

Some comparative fonts

SERIF	SANS SERIF	DECORATIVE
Times	Univers	*Brush Script*
Bembo	Avant Garde	**Benguiat Frisky**
Bookman Old Style	Futura	Chaucer
Cheltenham	Helvetica Narrow	**Broadway**
Garamond	Eurostile	
Palatino		
Times New Roman		

(All the above examples are the same point size – 14 point. Notice that although all are in 14 point, their relative heights and lengths are different.)

Comparative point sizes

Point size 8 is too small for the general text

Point size 10 is acceptable if you want to conserve space

Point size 12 is the normal size for both sans serif and serif fonts and is easily read

Point 14 and Point 16 can be used for subtitle headings

Point 18 and Point 20 and above should be reserved for titles and main headings

Figure 9.5 *Comparative fonts and point sizes*

first word is at the left margin) follows on from the preceding one, but the first word is indented by either one or two spaces.

Sometimes paragraphs can be started with letters – (a), (B) – or numbers – 1., (2), or III – the choice usually depending on your preferred or culture style of writing. Some writers use bullets to start paragraphs, but this can have the effect of reducing the number of impactive effects available for use throughout a document.

Headings

In addition to paragraphs documents are usually divided into sections, with the start of the different sections having different forms of heading. The first heading in the document is usually centred across the page and is in bold, upper case, of 14 or 16 point. The font for this main heading or title can be sans serif, if the remainder of the document is to be in serif font:

THE MAIN HEADING OR TITLE

Subheadings for the next level down, the headings for major sections, are usually in upper case but in a smaller font to the main title, placed either centrally or left aligned:

THE FIRST LEVEL SUBHEADING

or

THE FIRST LEVEL SUBHEADING

or

THE FIRST LEVEL SUBHEADING

Within sections of the text there will be frequently subsections: these will usually be headed in the font used in the first level headings, in bold but in lower case and in the point size of the first level heading, frequently with upper case for the start of each main word in the subheading, although this is not always the case. The subheadings can be centred or left aligned:

The Second Level Sub-Heading

or

The second level sub-heading

or

The second level sub-heading

If there are further subsections headings can be the same as for the second level, but with upper case for the first word only or, sometimes, the text can follow on the same line as the subhead:

The third level subheading. Here the text follows on rather than being displaced by a line space.

These are the conventions followed by many writers and publishers, but by no means all, and you do not need to follow any of them in your handouts as long as your meanings are clear and the text is understandable and has impact. But be consistent.

Grammatical construction

The rules for grammatical presentation and construction in the English language are many and complicated and this is not the place to describe or comment on them – reference books abound and it is recommended that you read and/or refer to these. A very readable and usable set of 14 booklets is published by Mandarin Books in association with the *Sunday Times*. But don't let the constraints of grammar override the need to make a clear, concise, readable and impactive handout. The rules will help to ensure that you do not make serious mistakes that will interfere with the effectiveness of the handout. The various punctuation marks do have an impact on the written word – commas, colons, semi-colons, etc all have their uses and the sense of a passage can be changed significantly by their misuse. But you are not setting out to produce a literary masterpiece – simply one that will satisfy the retention and recall aspects of the learning for the learners.

Remember that there are people who take the greatest delight in pointing out perhaps pedantic constructions, for the sake of doing so, and ignoring the message in which the construction is contained.

Some guidelines include the following.

- Don't try to make handouts grammatical, literary masterpieces – within the constraints of transferring the spoken to the written word, write as you talk.
- Within the guidance of the previous item, use language that is as simple as possible and appropriate to the context.
- Use 'I', 'You' and 'We' rather than 'One' and 'They'.
- Use the active rather than the passive form of verbs.
- Use short sentences – but be careful: too many of them, especially if they are too short, do not read easily and can be annoying.

- Use paragraphs that are as short as possible within a meaningful construction.
- Avoid dramatization – stick to the facts.
- Don't write in a pompous manner, trying to impress the reader – you won't.
- Use as few words as possible – KISS.
- Avoid clichés.
- Watch out for over-repetition of your favourite words.

GRAPHS, TABLES AND CHARTS IN HANDOUTS

The difficulties of using some of these graphics, particularly tables, on visual aids has been discussed; few of these problems relate to handouts as they can be examined closely and at leisure. If figures or text are printed in a reasonable size, any form of table or chart can be used. But the criterion remains – keep tables as clear and as simple as possible. A large, complicated table will not attract examination and its value will be lost. Obviously there will be occasions when simplicity in a table will not be possible and you may have to consider other forms of presentation, principal among which are:

- TABLES
- PIE CHARTS
- BAR AND COLUMN CHARTS
- LINE GRAPHS
- DECISION OR LOGICAL TREES

Most of these formats have several variations, a number of which are suitable for inclusion in handouts.

Tables

Tables can be valuable vehicles for demonstrating numerical inform-ation and their advantages include:

- more and greater detail can be used compared with, for example, OHP slides
- the handout can be studied at the reader's leisure and fine detail can be examined; this does not mean, however, that you should

go overboard when producing your handouts – the principle of KISS still applies
- they are easy to prepare
- variables can be shown and compared, such as the variations over time, etc.

The principal disadvantages are that:

- without strict control it is easy to include too much material and more than is necessary
- with a mass of information, even in the smaller tables, it can be difficult to identify significant and important parts.

In Chapter 5 when we were considering the use of charts, etc in OHP slides, the reproduction of data tables was discouraged: the handout is a place where they can be used – but remember KISS. Tables 9.1, 9.2 and 9.3 contain tabular data in three forms for comparison. Table 9.1 is Table 5.1 with details for three types of Unit Trust sales, with totals, over 11 years.

Table 9.1 *Examples of full table*

UNIT TRUST PURCHASES (11-YEAR TABLE)

Millions of currency units

Year	Ordinary	Special	Complex	Total
1970	104,883	29,169	12,888	146,940
1971	110,322	34,088	14,000	158,410
1972	113,992	31,066	14,092	159,150
1973	128,534	36,304	14,308	179,146
1974	148,024	47,468	14,624	210,116
1975	186,970	47,170	14,592	248,732
1976	187,386	52,438	14,156	253,980
1977	189,388	61,636	14,102	265,126
1978	207,888	72,954	13,348	294,190
1979	227,000	78,658	12,908	318,566
1980	245,960	94,006	13,210	353,176
Totals	1,850,347	584,957	152,228	2,587,532

Even in a handout this detail starts to become too much to read – such detail would be satisfactory for a company report, but not for a handout. If it is possible to reduce the detail mass, even by dividing the full table into sections, this will help.

Table 9.2 is the original table reduced to a section of five years, making the size and detail much more acceptable.

Table 9.2 *Example of sectioned table*

UNIT TRUST PURCHASES (FIVE-YEAR TABLE)

Millions of currency units

Year	Ordinary	Special	Complex	Total
1970	104,883	29,169	12,888	146,940
1971	110,322	34,088	14,000	158,410
1972	113,992	31,066	14,092	159,150
1973	128,534	36,304	14,308	179,146
1974	148,024	47,468	14,624	210,116
Totals	605,755	178,095	69,912	853,762

The third table, Table 9.3, includes this same material, but in a framed and grid-lined format, concentrating attention to individual parts of the table.

Table 9.3 *Example of framed table*

UNIT TRUST PURCHASES (FIVE-YEAR TABLE)				
Millions of currency units				
Year	Ordinary	Special	Complex	Total
1970	104,883	29,169	12,888	146,940
1971	110,322	34,088	14,000	158,410
1972	113,992	31,066	14,092	159,150
1973	128,534	36,304	14,308	179,146
1974	148,024	47,468	14,624	210,116
Totals	605,755	178,095	69,912	853,762

Pie charts

Pie charts, subdivided circles showing the breakdown of data, are popular alternatives to tables for presenting numerical information, as they satisfy the interest in graphical representation and also are quite different from any other form of chart. Figures 5.4 and 5.5 in Chapter 5 demonstrate straightforward, clear pie charts, standard and exploded, that are suitable for projection as OHP slides. Pie charts included in handouts can take these as their bases and introduce variations that make the chart more interesting. These variations might not be suitable for OHP slides because they might detract from the clarity. A typical example of such a variation is to draw the pie chart in a 3-D version.

Figure 9.6 demonstrates this conversion to 3-D for both a standard chart, and an exploded chart.

Figure 9.6   *3-D pie chart variations*

The advantages of pie charts include:

■ useful for demonstrating proportion differences
■ divisions of the data are clearly shown
■ colours can be used to emphasize the divisions
■ emphasis on particular divisions can be made by exploding the pie
■ pie charts appear attractive and different from other, more traditional charts.

Disadvantages include:

■ difficulty in drawing circles and dividing them into segments accurately
■ difficulty of converting the original data into percentages then into degrees.

These two disadvantages have been reduced considerably with the introduction of computer-generated PIE charts. There are many computer programs, usually associated with spreadsheets, that translate data into chart form, performing the calculations and drawing the chart itself. The variations shown in Figure 9.6 were produced in this way, very quickly and with little skill required.

Bar charts

Bar charts consist of vertical or horizontal bars, blocks and sometimes lines whose height or length represents the numerical value of the original data. Usually the bars are separated from each other, but they can be cumulative so that one bar can represent a number of pieces of data, perhaps the final size of the bar being the total of the data. Obviously these charts can come in a variety of forms. Figures 5.6 and 5.7 demonstrate the simple vertical bar chart (sometimes referred to as column charts) and the horizontal format respectively. As with the pie charts, these need to be kept simple for clear projection as an OHP slide, but greater variations can be included in bar charts produced for handouts – particularly with the help of the computer. Figure 9.7 shows a simple, vertical bar chart in 3-D form, a more attractive format than the flat, 2-D variety.

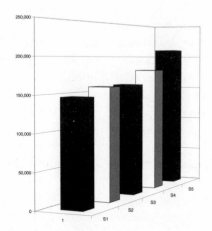

Figure 9.7 *3-D vertical bar chart*

The advantages of bar charts in handouts include:

■ useful for comparing both size and proportion
■ flexible
■ simplicity of format

- ease of drawing – all straight lines
- clear representation even when a number of pieces of data are compared
- the use of colour to separate the bars clearly.

There are few disadvantages, possibly the only complaint being that bar charts do not show as much information as tables and line graphs, but this is negated to a large extent by their simplicity and impact.

Line graphs

These are familiar to most people and can be valuable instruments to convert data into graphic images. They consist basically of two axes at right angles to each other, each axis being used for a different feature, eg time against amount, sale quantities against types of goods, etc. Figure 5.8 shows a simple line graph comparing the value of unit sales against time in years. Figure 5.9 extends this representation and includes, on the one graph, information relating to the three different forms of unit. Marking the intersecting points for each value, eg 100,000 at 1970; 190,000 at 1977; 250,000 at 1980 and so on produces the line. Straight lines drawn between the points then join the value marks. The intervening space, although represented by a straight line, shows the movement during the period of time. The joining lines can in fact be smoothed into curves, but this introduces unnecessary difficulties. The lines can also follow the 'line of best fit' in widely scattered points, this being referred to as a scatter graph.

Line graphs can be produced in a much greater variety than the two examples shown in Chapter 5, although there are a number of 'rules' as well as possible variations.

- The vertical axis is referred to as the y-axis and the horizontal one as the x-axis.
- The x-axis is used for an independent variable, usually time when this is one of the factors involved.
- The line of the graph progresses from left to right on the horizontal axis and from bottom to top on the vertical axis.
- Unless the graph would be unnecessarily condensed into the upper part, the starting point for the vertical scale should be zero – otherwise the graph can distort or misrepresent the data.
- The vertical axis scale should not be extended relative to the horizontal axis scale, as this misrepresents the data, making the peaks and troughs over obvious and misleading.

Ensuring that the vertical and horizontal axes are correct relative to each other is the most difficult aspect of effective graph production. Variations of these are also used to deliberately misrepresent data. Another misrepresentation method commonly used is to be highly selective about the period of time to be compared, starting, for example, the year after the worst year in a series.

Approaches to the production of line graphs are similar to those of the other chart forms:

- the computer making the transfer from data to chart much easier than by hand
- coloured lines being used to make the separation of data clearer
- line formats varied (–––, --------, ..., xxxxxxxxx, ********* being typical examples)
- different point marks (•, ✖, ●, ○, ■, □, *, ◆, +, and so on).

These simple variations can work against the clarity of the graph if too many are included and too many lines are shown on the graph. Using various colours, lines and point marks, you can distinguish fairly clearly up to eight variables. Even this number may be too many, particularly if the graph is small and if several variable lines run close to each other or cross each other a number of times.

Combined charts

There is no reason why more than one form of chart should not be combined, either to demonstrate two different effects on the same chart, or to make important points about the information by reinforcing them with a superimposed chart. Figure 9.8 demonstrates a combined chart of a simple line graph superimposed on a bar chart.

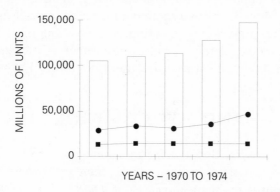

Figure 9.8 *A combined chart*

Decision or logical trees

Charts that are frequently used in or as handouts do not have to be in the form of comparison charts, such as bar, line and pie charts. One different form is the decision or logical tree, otherwise known as an algorithm. This is used to reach a solution by taking the problem-solver through a series of logical steps to the decision. The approach is basically the same as happens within a computer when questions requiring 'yes' and 'no' answers are asked, the response leading to another 'yes/no' question.

Figure 9.9 demonstrates one of these decision trees with a problem for a dental receptionist dealing with a patient. At strategic points in the tree questions are posed requiring a 'yes' or 'no' answer. The receptionist is led along the appropriate path depending on the answer: at the end of this path another question is asked requiring the 'yes' or 'no' response, and so on. In the decision tree complex textual descriptions of a procedure can be simplified and presented in a more easily comprehensible and recallable form. In such cases, the tree is ideal material for a handout, either with supporting text or as a stand-alone training aid.

HANDOUT ISSUE

We have looked at when to issue handouts – before the session; during the session; at the end of the session; at the end of the course. Whenever you issue yours, avoid making it appear that the handouts are unconnected pieces of paper that can easily become dog eared, be torn, lost or forgotten about. The simplest way to do this is to issue the learners with a ring-binder, holepunch all the handouts and suggest that they file the handouts within the binder. This binder can serve a number of other functions – as a container for the course call-up papers; a record of the pre-briefing meeting; a statement of the course objectives; Log Books; activity briefs; questionnaires, etc, so that the binder becomes a permanent record of the course and what happened.

HANDOUT CONTROL

If you, or the training department in which you work, handles a significant number of training programmes, there will be a vast number of handouts around. Problems then arise in *finding* relevant OHP slides and handouts. Suggestions were made in Chapter 5 about the control

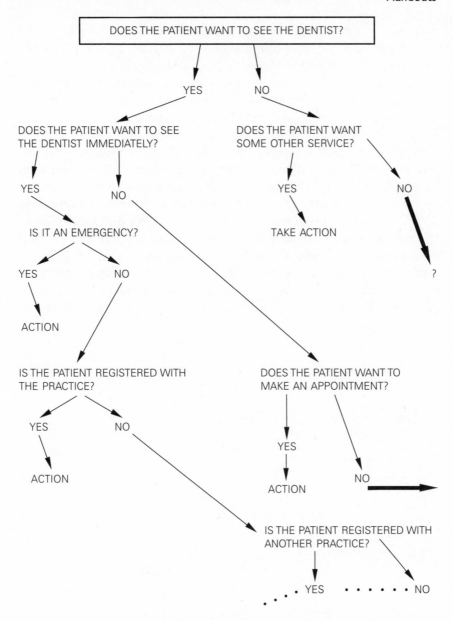

Figure 9.9 *A decision tree or algorithm*

of OHP transparencies. Handouts will probably be in two formats – paper copies and master disks for the computer.

If a running stock of handouts is to be maintained, the normal method is to file these in course batches in folders, clearly titled as to their contents. This is satisfactory if a particular handout is used on one course only, but if any are multipurpose they can be kept in a separate master file with dummy folders referring to the master file placed in the course file.

Computer production of handouts usually results in the handout files being saved on floppy disks rather than the internal hard disk; as a consequence a substantial number of disks can mount up. These can be filed in a similar way to hard copy – in course-related files or a master file with supplementary slave files for course handouts. Several methods of filing and noting the disks are available and you will wish to use the one used in your organization or the one that you prefer. My method is to keep all handouts relating to a course on one disk, which includes a contents list. I also have a master disk that contains dummy files (also indexed) that relate to handouts that can be used on several courses, and a disk that catalogues the locations. This is a successful method for me, but I have to be careful to keep the entries up to date. Control can be maintained by always having a reference code for each handout, including the date when it was produced or last modified.

10

Other Training and Learning Aids – 1

Training and learning can be aided and supported in much wider ways than those described so far, and this chapter and the next will present a selection of these. It could be said that everything the trainer does or makes available to the learner – techniques, material, approach – is an aid to learning, otherwise no learning takes place. However, this description is too broad for our purposes, as to include everything would be to write a book covering *every* aspect of training and learning – a daunting task.

If we take the basic approach to providing a training event so that learning can take place, the core event will be the straight input or lecture by the trainer, devoid of visual aids or any other supportive device. Any of the aids discussed hitherto that are added will enhance (or even replace) the input. But these can be supplemented by techniques and instruments that are well within the field of training and learning aids. These will include:

- NOTETAKING
- ACTIVITIES, GAMES, EXERCISES
- BUZZ AND DISCUSSION GROUPS
- CASE STUDIES AND SIMULATIONS
- OBSERVATION INSTRUMENTS

Notetaking, activities, buzz/discussion groups, and case studies/ simulations will be discussed in this chapter, observation instruments in Chapter 11.

NOTETAKING

Handouts were described in the previous chapter as written training aids that could be used at different stages of the learning process. These aids are produced by the trainer prior to the training event and represent summaries of the material that was intended to be included in the training. However, learners are individuals with singular views on how they learn and what they accept as learning, and handouts may be either used or ignored, used as learning and recall aids alone or require other supportive aids. The last named are usually the personal notes made by the learner during the session. Hopefully these reflect the messages included in a handout (expressed in the learner's own terms and language), and also the training messages expressed during the session.

The argument can be raised that if there is a clear, effective handout there is no need for the learners to make what are repetitive notes. However, people learn and recall in different ways and it appears that there is a large group who feel they have to make notes as a learning aid and who in fact learn more effectively as a result. Many take this to the extent of insisting on taking notes even when a specific announcement is made that handouts will be available – perhaps they do not trust the handouts to include everything they require!

I am included in this group, and find I learn more effectively if I write notes, even if it just summarizing and rephrasing the existing material. If I just listen to a speaker or read some text there is less chance of my recalling as much of the contribution than if I make my own notes. Many people who do this comment that they do not look at the notes again. However, this may not be significant, as the notetaking has performed its function of reinforcing the learning at the time.

Forms of notetaking

The particular form of notetaking depends on the preferences of the individuals, a number of different ways being evident. However, as commented above, many notetakers say they rarely look at the notes after the event. One of the principal reasons for this is certainly the form in which the notes are written. Many notes are scribbled, untidy and frequently contain more material than the related handout. Consequently the first sight of the notes after the event is sufficient to put them out of sight!

This need not necessarily be so as, with a little care, notes can be produced in a form that will encourage reference to them. The criteria must be clarity, and above all, brevity. The longer the material, the less encouragement there is to read it.

THE PRINCIPAL METHODS OF MAKING NOTES

There are four principal methods:

- THE TRADITIONAL, VERTICAL METHOD
- THE HEADLINE METHOD
- THE HORIZONTAL APPROACH
- PATTERNED NOTES

THE TRADITIONAL, VERTICAL METHOD

This is the most common form of notetaking, with which most people are familiar and which most people use. The range of its effective use is wide, ranging from scrappy, almost unreadable scribbles to very full notes, clear and literate (although many of these are the products of rewriting from the original scribbles). The reason for the scribbling is easily understood: apart from using shorthand or other speedwriting, few people can write legibly as fast as the speaker talks or even as fast as their own brain working. Consequently the choice is between writing slowly and clearly and as a result perhaps missing some of what is being said, or scribbling down as much as possible. Neither choice is desirable and the 'scribbling' is in the vast majority of cases best left for notes that will be rewritten.

Abbreviations

If you are intent on using this approach, the use of your own form of shorthand and abbreviations can help to speed the process. This technique can, of course, be used in other forms of notes.

Some simple abbreviations you can use include:

+ or & – and	ε – the speed version of
y – why	e or E
u – you	ur – your
b – be	r – are
c – see or sea	q – queue
/ – divide or divided	* – multiply
I – one	2 – to or too
4 – for	-g – 'ing' ending
	-n – 'ion' ending

Remember also the standard abbreviations or literary conventions in common use:

eg – for example	ie – that is
∵ – because	∴ – therefore
cf – compare(d) with	= – equals, is the same as
≅ – approximately equals	→ – lead to, progress to
≠ – not the same as, does not equal	> – is greater than
< – is less than	

The following guidance suggests some helpful approaches to this technique.

Division into paras and sub-paras

As each specific part of the session unfolds, it is helpful to divide the notes into paragraphs and sub-paragraphs, if possible each with a headline, not for any grammatical or aesthetic reasons but to make the different parts of the note clearer visually.

Underlining for emphasis

It is essential in this note form to make the different words, phrases and sentences as separate and as visually impactive as possible. Underlining, either single or double can be used to make these parts stand out. However, as with any technique used to highlight parts of the notes, use the underlining sparingly or you will find that the impact is lost when too many parts are treated in this manner.

Colours for emphasis

Bold and different colours can be used as another method for producing emphasis in the notes, although this requires a bit of juggling. Coloured pens can be used or, if the idea of using several pens is too daunting, colour can be added to monocolour by the use of highlighter pens. This highlighting can replace the need to underline. Different colours can be used for alternate paragraphs (or sections) to increase the separation emphasis.

Framing for emphasis or isolation

> **Another simple technique for emphasising sections of the notes is to box or frame the relevant parts, emphasis being increased even more if the box lines or the words are in a different colour to those around them.**

Again, the use of boxes and framing should be controlled so that they are not used too much, thus neutralizing the effect.

THE HEADLINE METHOD

This technique is a variation of the traditional full notes method and involves cutting out many of the words that would normally be entered and using a shorthand or key word form only.

As the session develops, it should be possible to identify the key sections that make up the content. Frequently the speaker signals the change from one key area to another by the use of a summary OHP slide of the previous section, or a slide announcing the content of the next section. At these stages, identify the section with a key word or phrase written in block capitals (perhaps in a colour, underlined or boxed).

As the section is developed, add further key words in lower case writing. These words should be as few as possible, being limited to those that will act as triggers to your memory when you eventually read the notes. Different people will obviously include a different number of words, but the criterion remains to limit them to as few as possible. Because you have to listen carefully to identify the key ideas, and you are not writing a lot, you will be able to listen more effectively to the speaker: this, linked with your key notes, should consolidate your understanding, recall and learning of the material being presented. If there is also a handout to the session, the use of this, your key notes and your memory recall will make it an effective learning experience, more so than without the support of the learning aid notes.

THE HORIZONTAL APPROACH

This method breaks away from the traditional approach of using the vertical placement of your notes on what usually become several sheets of A4 paper. Instead it uses the more natural, horizontal way that the mind works and produces the notes, frequently on one sheet of paper only.

The technique is very similar to the vertical method, except that you start with your blank sheet of paper laid horizontally in front of you. Key headlines are entered as previously, but instead of these following each other vertically down the paper they are entered horizontally.

The first key headline is written in the top left corner of the paper. As the secondary key words and phrases in that section are identified these are entered underneath the key headline. The next section headline is placed immediately to the right of the first headline, with its associated key words, etc placed below it. And so on across the paper.

This method introduces what can be a further discipline on you to control the amount of words you note. Because the aim is to constrain the note to one side of the A4 sheet you will find that this is in the back of your mind as you write and you automatically try to keep the words to a minimum. However, do not let this interfere with your need to produce an understandable and usable note.

Of course, as again only headlines are included, the notetaker must be fully aware of what needs to be written about each item, but this must be weighed against the alternative of a mass of scribbled words that may be of little help.

PATTERNED NOTES

The patterned-note method was pioneered by Tony Buzan and is basically a variation, albeit a radical one, of the key word approach.

This approach has a number of advantages once you become accustomed to working in this medium but, although valuable, it is not as easy to come to terms with as the other methods.

At the start of the session you should place in the central box the key word or phrase being noted for the session. The first branches emanating from this box are annotated with the key words or phrases relating to the main subject areas as they emerge during the session. Sub-ideas are then added, branching out from the main branches to which they relate.

Colours, boxes, symbols (eg ?, *, ➔, ⬅------➔, ☺, 📄, 🖥, ☞), directions – 'OHP', 'Issue h/o' etc – topic linking lines and so on can be added, particularly in different colours in order to make them stand out.

Figure 10.1 illustrates a simple example of part of a patterned note. I find that when I am constructing a pattern single words are not sufficient for me; I need a phrase or sentence to remind me of the particular concept being recorded. But a patterned note is a very personal production, one that can often be understood only by the person who produced it. If necessary, therefore, the notes from the pattern can be converted to one of the more traditional formats.

ACTIVITIES

An activity in the training and development sense refers to a practical, experiential event in which the learners participate, rather than their sitting back in a passive mode, such as listening to a lecture. Such events are described loosely as activities, games, or exercises: your use may be from personal choice, but my preference is for 'activities' as a cover-all word. 'Game' suggests a less than serious learning intention, a pastime or spare-time event, and 'exercise' can be too suggestive of the classroom.

Features

The features of an activity are as follows.

- It provides a vehicle for learning, with the learners *doing* something from which the relevant lessons can be drawn.
- The experience can be based on a real-life situation or an artificially produced event.

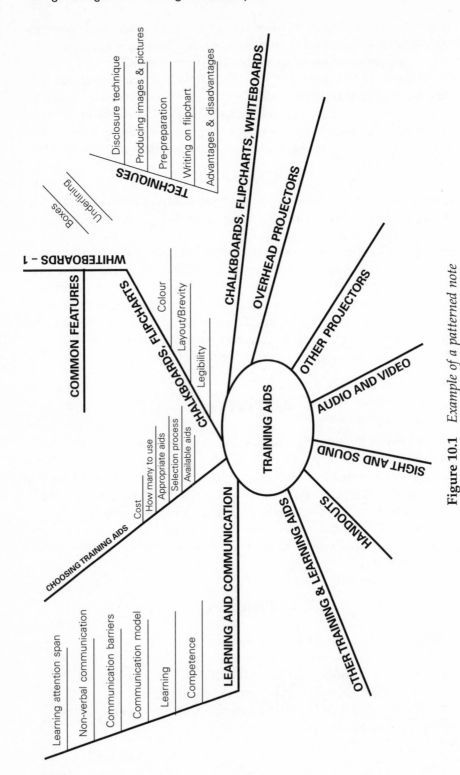

Figure 10.1 *Example of a patterned note*

- Appropriate activities can be selected to suit the learning event, the learners, the environment, the numbers involved and the time available.
- The common feature is that the learners, either as the learning group or divided into sub-groups, perform the event either in their own personae or in selected roles.
- The details of the event are summarized in a brief or set of briefs that might be fully detailed or simple summaries from which the learners can develop an appropriate role.
- The activity can be observed in a range of ways.
- Generally, learners enjoy taking part in activities and consequently the likelihood of learning is enhanced.
- They can be used as learning activities, introductions, icebreakers or session shakers.

Disadvantages

- There is a danger for too many activities to be included in a programme, with the result that the event might come to be known as the 'game show'.
- Not all learners will learn, or want to learn from the activity approach.
- Some learners might see the activity as 'playing silly games'.

ACTIVITY USES

There are four principal uses for activities in training and development programmes.

```
■ LEARNING ACTIVITY
■ INTRODUCTION
■ ICEBREAKER
■ SESSION SHAKER
```

Learning activity

This is the main use of an activity during a training and development programme and is used to:

- demonstrate, prior to more defined learning approaches, learning points about the subject under consideration, eg an activity prior to a detailed input session to enable the learners to identify the level of their existing knowledge and skills
- consolidate, through practice, learning that has been achieved prior to the activity in some other form of training approach, eg an input session.

These two uses immediately suggest that there can be more than one activity, at different times, within a training session. For example, a training session might follow the pattern below.

1. A brief, input introduction to the subject by the trainer, including a general description and statement of learning objectives.
2. An activity related to the session material to demonstrate and assess the level of the learners' knowledge and skill at this stage.
3. An input of the new material by the trainer, using relevant audio and visual aids and encouraging active participation by the learners through questioning and discussion.
4. At relevant point(s) during the session, mini activities might be held to clarify particular points, eg by means of buzz groups (see later).
5. An activity, real-life based or artificially produced to consolidate the learning, and enable the learners to practise the learning points.
6. A full discussion of the activity and the learning points for the session.

Introduction

Almost every training course benefits from some form of participant introduction activity at the start of the event. In very short events this introduction can be brief, but in longer events, particularly where participant interaction is important, the initial introductions can be quite complex and extended. Whatever form of introduction activity is used, although the emergent information is useful and important, the real importance of the activity is getting the learners involved from an early stage.

Introduction activities include:

- the traditional 'creeping death', in which, in turn, the members introduce themselves, either on a free basis or following topic guidelines suggested by the trainer

- the 'Russian roulette' variation in which the trainer nominates, at random, the order in which the learners should introduce themselves
- paired interviewing and introductions where, in pairs, the learners interview each other then introduce their partner to the full group
- progressive group introductions, in which small groups introduce themselves within the group, then change groups and repeat the process, until everybody has been introduced to everybody else
- identity maps in which the learners draw pictures illustrating their lives and careers and use these to introduce themselves
- identity wheels which have segments requiring the entry of information by the learners about themselves.

It is all too easy for the trainer to select the 'Creeping Death' approach, even when there is time to include something more adventurous, but this is the introduction activity that is least enjoyed by the learners and is usually less effective than others.

Icebreakers

Icebreakers are activities that link closely with introductions and usually follow an initial introduction activity. The introductions are intended to activate the learners and start the process of enabling them to relate with each other. Icebreakers continue this process, opening up even further the reactions of the participants to each other. The introductions have started the process of encouraging the learners to divulge information about themselves; the icebreaker continues and develops this process.

Two types of icebreaker exist: one for the purpose described above; the other much simpler in that it aims to make the participants feel more at ease with each other.

The latter activity can take almost any form, many of which have no relation to work or to the training. This type of activity can be a simple problem-solving one or can be a much deeper one involving the development of trust by means of a Trust Walk. In a Trust Walk the participants develop trust in each other by, for example, going for a walk in which they are blindfolded in turn and not allowed to communicate verbally. Quizzes held in sub-groups are common in this context, as activities that encourage cooperation, but in an atmosphere of fun.

The deeper icebreakers try to enable further information about the participants to emerge. An example of this is the Expectations or Hopes/Concerns chart described in Chapter 3.

Session shakers

Session shakers, or energizers, are generally simple activities, short and sharp, that usually have no relationship to the programme objectives. They can be introduced at any time during a programme, the trigger being a flagging energy level within the learning group. A useful switch during a programme is when it is becoming 'heavy' or it has required the expenditure of a lot of mental effort. Here a physical session shaker activity can be introduced. Or, conversely, when the session has been physical, the activity can require the group to sit down and take part in a relatively passive mental activity.

Many session shakers have their origins in children's or party games, or variations of physical education exercises. Several are variations on competitive relay activities – for example, words on cards taken across a room to the remainder of the team by a member hopping. When something has been done with this word, another member hops across the room to pick up another word and return to the team.

PLANNING AND PREPARING ACTIVITIES

Activities should be planned and prepared as carefully as any other training approach, even though during the event they may appear to be spontaneous. Icebreakers and session shakers, in particular, are usually given a spontaneous appearance, and their introduction may in fact be just that. But the trainer must be prepared before the event with a supply of such activities to be introduced whenever the atmosphere of the programme demands this.

Planning

When you are planning your training programme, the question of the use of activities as aids to learning should be considered. You should ask yourself the following questions.

- What are my objectives for this training programme?
- What type of approach am I going to use?
- What type of learning opportunities am I going to include?
- Specifically, do I want to and/or need to include activities?
- Have I the programme time to include them?
- Why; how many; what; how; when?

The final questions of why, how many, etc are practical questions to be asked once the use of activities has been decided on, and will lead to justification for their use.

Preparation

Once the decision has been made about the inclusion of different types of activities in the programme, preparations for their use should be made as far as possible, according to the nature of the activity. Consider the following preparation checklist.

1. Be as familiar as possible with the activity – its form, timing, operation, review and feedback.
2. If the activity is new to you, try it out with a group of colleagues or other 'safe' group.
3. Produce the necessary briefs, instruction sheets, observation and review/feedback instruments.
4. Check that you have any other resources required by the activity.
5. If the activity is physical, confirm that it is suitable for the particular group.
6. If relevant, decide how you are going to form the activity sub-groups.
7. Check that you have sufficient space for a group to perform the activity, and/or additional rooms if multiple sub-groups are to be involved.
8. Check any safety factors necessary.
9. Confirm the activity timings – this can be done in conjunction with (2) above, bearing in mind that experienced trainers might perform the activity more quickly than learners.
10. Prepare your verbal introduction for the activity.
11. Decide on the observation strategy and methods.
12. Decide what role you will take during the activity.
13. Decide the methods for reviewing the activity and giving feedback.

Briefs and instruction sheets

Many activities are too complex and complicated for a simple verbal introduction to the learning groups to be sufficient. This means that role briefs or individual and group instruction sheets should be provided for the participants at the start of the activity.

The preparation of effective briefs is not easy. If they are long and complex, understanding may be impeded; if they are short and snappy, there may be insufficient information to help the participants. The dummy-run recommended above should help you to achieve a balance, although the 'ineffectiveness' of the brief will always be used as an excuse by participants who 'fail' in an activity.

Figure 10.2 shows an example of a short brief given to a number of sub-groups to decide which learning subjects should be included in the following day's programme, and Figure 10.3 shows an even shorter (but still effective for the activity purpose) brief. It is in fact so short that 'analysis' has deliberately not been defined.

LEARNING DECISION

The following topics are available for tomorrow. You have 30 minutes to decide as a group which four topics you would prefer to be included. Be prepared to present your selection to the other groups with reasons for your selection. A final decision will be made in the full group, return to the sub-groups being arranged if necessary.

Topics:

A.................................... B ....

C.................................... D ....

E.................................... F ....

G .... H ....

I .... J ....

Figure 10.2 *A short brief*

CAR PARK ANALYSIS

You have 20 minutes to produce an analysis of the cars in the car park. Write your findings on a sheet of flipchart paper and be prepared to discuss these with the other groups.

Figure 10.3 *An even shorter brief*

BUZZ AND DISCUSSION GROUPS

One of the most effective training aids is to shift the role of the learner from a passive to an active role – the activity is a good example of this. An active role for the learners means their greater engagement in the training and learning process. Another method of achieving this is to have the learners take part in some form of discussion, whether led by the trainer or, preferably, run by themselves.

BUZZ GROUPS

Buzz groups are the simplest form of discussion to set up and use, although this does not necessarily mean that they can be used only with small groups.

Buzz groups are normally used during an input session when the trainer feels that, in order to aid the training process, the learners should become involved in the process. The session may have reached a point where a controversial subject has been raised, or it would be useful to obtain the range of views held in the group.

Here, the trainer suspends the input and suggests that the learning group might consider X. To do this the group is divided into several small groups, the size and number depending on the size of the whole group. Rather than send the groups to various rooms to carry out their discussions, they are asked simply to move their chairs around so that they form more or less isolated groups, all in the one room. The groups are advised of the time they have available and are recommended to select a reporter who will report back to the full group the results of the group's discussion. This selection of reporters is an important aspect, as the reporter is not expressing his or her own views but, in a neutral role, those of the group. This exemption from the expression of personal views usually helps the individuals to speak more easily.

Use and objectives

The objectives and use of buzz groups are to:

- Add variety to a session
- Encourage the learners to discuss
- Encourage quieter members to speak
- Give practice in reporting back
- Enable a large number of views to emerge in a short time
- Enable a variety of views to be expressed
- Enable members to learn from each other
- Preserve anonymity of views

Reviewing

After the buzz group it is necessary to bring the sub-groups together again in the larger learning group to enable reports, feedback and reviews to take place. As the buzz group process is simple, the review process should also be kept simple. Some guidelines, however, will be helpful.

1. At the end of the buzz, let the participants stay where they are in their groups – this will encourage them to relate to what their reporter is saying and maintains the development of interactions in the group.
2. Ask the spokesperson to report first, then ask the other members of the buzz group if they have anything to add.
3. Give every buzz group the opportunity to report.
4. If a number of issues have been discussed, ask each group in turn to comment on the first issue, avoiding repetition of comments already made. For the next round of reporting change the order of speaking to avoid a group 'creeping death'.
5. Encourage the groups to challenge each other's views, as this can frequently result in a building of the original statement.
6. Wherever possible, write up the views on a flipchart that can be retained and posted on the training room wall.
7. Don't be afraid to intervene as necessary, asking questions of clarification or probing for a fuller statement, or to control the excess contributions of one group.
8. In successive buzz groups you will need to decide whether to retain the original grouping or mix the members. The former approach helps to develop group/team entities and interrelationships, whereas the latter may help to ensure a wider sharing of views.

DISCUSSION GROUPS

These are well known and well used in training programmes and are training aids that can be viewed as extensions of the buzz group. Discussion groups can be formed and used in a variety of ways, as shown in the following box.

FORMATION	USES
FULL TRAINING GROUP	INVOLVING ALL MEMBERS ACTIVELY
SUB-GROUPS	WIDE SHARING OF INFORMATION, etc
PRE-COURSE SELECTION	PROBLEM SOLVING AND DECISION
SELECTION FROM CRITERIA	MAKING
GROUP SELF-SELECTION	PRACTISING DISCUSSION SKILLS
PRE-COURSE DETERMINATION	VARYING TRAINING METHODS AND
DEMONSTRATION	PACE
INSTANTANEOUS FORMATION	

Discussion groups, as opposed to buzz groups, are not commonly instantaneously formed events, although this can and does happen. Care has to be taken with spontaneous discussions as they start with ill-defined objectives and have a habit of carrying on longer than intended. Most discussions, whether involving the learners as a full group or as working sub-groups, have been planned during the course design period and are introduced by the trainer in a controlled manner. In the full group approach, depending on the objectives, the discussion can be led by the trainer or one of the participants, elected or selected for that purpose.

When discussions are to be held in sub-groups, similar to buzz groups but with a more formal set-up, various criteria can be used for selecting members for each group:

- selection by arbitrarily placing cut-off points around the group
- completely random selection
- formal selection from criteria – experience, behavioural patterns, age, sex, etc
- planned progression with learners in different groups as successive discussions are held
- self-selection within the full group.

Discussion demonstrations

One occasion when a discussion is a very specific training aid is during a training event aimed specifically at discussion skills. This is the demonstration of a discussion event, usually run by the trainer along 'bad' lines.

The trainer selects a number of learners to form a discussion group – the selection might include a very quiet person, two very high contributors, at least one argumentative person, and a 'normal' member. The group holds the discussion in front of the remainder of the learners and during it the trainer/leader tries to demonstrate, and have performed by the members, all the 'bad' features of a discussion – a leader's dictatorial approach in choice of subject and approach; a leader's dominance of the discussion; a leader's confrontational disagreement with members; ignoring the quiet member; making and allowing interruptions; no summaries and an abrupt end, without thanks, to the event.

The demonstration would be followed by a full discussion in which the good and bad elements of the discussion would be identified, leading to a summary of points to avoid and those to follow. A 'good' demonstration can follow this, although it is normally preferable to encourage the good features in natural discussions that follow this stage.

The discussion leading brief

One aid that is recommended for use with the discussion group as a training aid itself is for the leader to construct, prior to the discussion, a brief for the content of the event. This attempts to ensure that everything relevant and important is included. There are two main forms of brief:

- the shopping list
- the pros and cons list.

The shopping list

This is a simple reminder laid out in whatever form (vertical, horizontal, pattern) best suits the user. It includes, in a clear form, key words that will remind you of the subjects that should be discussed – the training technique of *must knows, should knows, could knows* can be very useful here. During the discussion the items are ticked off as they are covered, the balance suggesting what has still to be discussed, individual items acting as useful prompts if the discussion falters.

The pros and cons list

When the discussion subject is controversial, or likely to arouse differences of viewpoint, the leader should be prepared for this by producing a pros and cons list prior to the event. This will include, in a summarized form, as many of the subject aspects and arguments as can be identified.

Divide a sheet of paper vertically, one side headed 'pros' and the other 'cons'. Enter in the relevant column all the points you have identified and, during the discussion, as with the shopping list, strike through the items as they are covered. This list is not only a reminder of what should be included in the discussion, but also a checklist of the main arguments that should emerge.

Planning and design

Planned discussions require substantial preparation if they are going to be effective as a training aid, and a suggested checklist for the leader/trainer is given below.

1. Decide on the topic – either a full subject or part of a larger subject.
2. Decide how to launch the discussion:
   - reference to previous material
   - a provocative statement
   - an extension of the current input
   - a visual aid showing the subject graphically.
3. Decide and write down your opening statement or quotation, to avoid a hesitant start.
4. Determine seating format – a circular arrangement is frequently the most effective for discussions.
5. Decide your own role.
   - initiator and prompter then withdrawal
   - active participant as leader or member
   - participant on invitation by the group.
6. Identify any special action that may be possible. For example, keep a note of any ideas or statements that you might throw into the discussion if it flags, or consider how you are going to control known dominating members.

7. Decide whether you are going to challenge untrue or unclear contributions yourself or whether you are going to leave this to the members themselves, and how you might encourage such challenges.

CASE STUDIES AND SIMULATIONS

Case studies and simulations are more substantial and complex than normal training activities and can be powerful aids to training and learning.

CASE STUDIES

Case studies provide full details of a task subject for the learners to consider, discuss and perform. A historical record of the background of the event or organization is provided, often including material that is not necessary for the completion of the task, but always including the essential data. The case and its data can be completely imaginary, constructed to ensure that the relevant learning points emerge, or can be based on a real organizational situation. The closer the case is to an obviously real event the more acceptable to the learners it will be.

With the case study data the learners are presented with a problem to solve; additional, newer data being made available, usually on request. The learners make recommendations for a solution to either the trainer, another group (when multigroups are operating) or to an invited person from the organization involved in the case study. The actual solution and the process by which it was reached will need to be discussed in this review.

Planning and design

Planning and design are essential if the case study is to be effective and steps will include decisions on:

1. whether the case will be artificial, based on a real event, or a description of the real event as it happened
2. the extent of the study – a complete organizational problem, specific managerial problems, or personal value situations

3. the resources to be made available. As suggested earlier, the data should be honest and complete, with no 'deliberate' mistakes included. Reports, organization charts, spreadsheets and job descriptions may be needed, possibly modified to make them suitable for the training situation
4. whether the case study should be complete, or perhaps broken up into several cases linked with the progress of the training event – data collection, analysis, problem solving, decision making, assessment and review. Physical resource needs and availability should also be assessed – briefs, computers, spreadsheet and word-processing software, calculators, flipcharts, etc
5. whether observers should be used, how and to what extent
6. the trainer(s)' role during the activity
7. the process points you and/or the observers should be looking for during the activity
8. the range of possible recommendations for the case solution
9. the format of the review process, including the roles of the trainer and the observers.

Learner requirements

The brief given to the learners will in many case studies be extensive and complex, and time must be given for them to assimilate this information because they will have to:

1. identify the problem, its location and extent
2. produce and agree optional approaches to the problem
3. agree on the internal organization of their group and the allocation of roles as necessary
4. be able to work together as an effective, interactive problem-solving group
5. understand the data and its implications
6. systematically collect and analyse the data and know when to seek additional information
7. produce in a systematic manner a range of possible solutions and identify the optimum solution from this range
8. recommend and present in the most effective manner their recommendations and be able to argue their case in the face of disagreement
9. identify, with the help of the trainer and observers, their process and the learning achieved from the case.

Reviewing the case study

An activity as important in learning terms as a case study demands that as much learning as possible is extracted for and by the learners. A substantial review period following the activity should go a long way to achieving these aims and sufficient time should be built into the programme to enable this. In most learning cases both the content and the activity process and behaviours will be considered, although in some cases only one or the other will enter the review.

The review should be built upon a range of questions and the task review questions should include the following.

- What data was analysed and how was it assessed to suggest the problem?
- How accurate was the group's analysis of the information?
- What was the problem that was identified?
- Were there any other problems?
- What did the group do or consider doing about these problems?
- To what extent was a range of possible solutions proposed?
- How did the group approach consideration of the range of possible solutions?
- What solution was recommended and why?
- To what extent was the implementation of the solution considered?

The checklist will also ask questions about the activity process.

- How did the group go about organizing itself and allocating roles?
- Were relevant experience and skills identified within the group?
- To what extent was all relevant information considered and did they take advantage of the additional information provided?
- Did the group miss any significant information and, if so, what was the result of this?
- If the group had a leader, to what extent was this leader successful in the role – why or why not?
- How well did the members of the group interact with each other?
- How were personal problems in the group resolved?
- How difficult did the group find the task, and in particular what aspects did they find more difficult than others?
- How readily did they approach the concept of the generation of more than one possible solution?
- How difficult did they find the decision making, and how were any problems resolved?

- What (and who) helped the success of the activity?
- What (and who) hindered the success of the activity?
- If the activity had to be repeated, what changes would be made?

SIMULATIONS

Simulations are very similar to case studies but are much more extensive, usually more complex and require the learners to take on individual roles, rather than only being part of a group (albeit a role-playing member of that group). They are working representations of real life, and attempt to model this in the safer world of a training and development programme. The learners take on real 'roles' – chief executive, marketing manager, operations manager, etc – and attempt to produce a simulation as near real life as possible.

The information given to the learners is more extensive than in the case study, relating to a complete, operating organization, for example one that is experiencing problems or needs to increase its market share. Computer and hard data is available for all aspects of the organization, and participants must analyse and act upon this data. Every attempt is made to replicate real environments, with the participants having separate rooms and communication links, and most simulations require:

- all paper resources – reports, financial statements, plans and vision statements
- simulation briefs for the learners
- a number of rooms
- computers installed with all relevant software
- video recorders and playback equipment
- working materials and stationery – telephones, faxes, copiers, calculators, and any other necessary office or situation equipment
- expert availability on an agreed basis
- trainer availability.

Usage

Simulations have a wide range of uses, in many cases the only restriction being the large scale of the event. Some uses can be:

- *Trainer development programmes* – this could involve, at the end of a development programme, a simulation in which a group or several sub-groups plan, design and implement a short training course incorporating the learning they had achieved.

■ *Management development* – this is the area in which simulations have a high potential with organizational operation being duplicated as described earlier.

■ *Skill practice, licence renewal* – probably the best-known example of this simulation area is the flight simulator for aircraft pilots. These are used for new pilots, the reassessment of existing pilots when new operational or equipment changes are introduced, or general updating training.

■ *General problem solving* – organizations other than industrial and commercial ones can be simulated, such as training for town and country planners. In this case the participants receive data relating to their particular requirements – maps, geological surveys, natural resources distribution data, existing and proposed population areas, communication factors, underground problems, etc.

Timing

One argument against simulations in training and development is the amount of resource, planning and design necessary, but the principal one must be the amount of time most simulations require. Even quite simple simulations require at least a day, and many need several days. In fact many simulations take the part of a full training and development programme, the simulation being the learning vehicle from which all the learning points can emerge.

Summary

The significant aspects of simulations as aids to training and development can be summarized as follows.

■ They are usually problem-solving activities modelled on real situations and environments.
■ Solutions are flexible (as in real life).
■ Participants perform roles that may or may not reflect their own job roles.
■ Roles can be selected by the trainer from: learner data (job, behaviour); the identified need of the learners to simulate other roles or behaviour; random allocation; or by self-selection (as part of the exercise).

- Prediction of the end result can be difficult, as progress will depend entirely on the learners.
- The simulation can often become real, with special relationships, emotions and feelings being generated during (and after!) the simulation.
- Simulations can range from the simple to the highly complex and can be people and organization based or skill related.
- Simulations are probably the most complex and difficult training activity to prepare and perform, but can be very rewarding for both learners and trainers.

11

Other Training and
Learning Aids – 2

This chapter continues the description of other training and learning aids and covers observation instruments.

OBSERVATION INSTRUMENTS

Unless the training programme consists completely of passive input sessions, a very large proportion of the learning achieved will be through experiential activities, role plays, simulations, etc. In order to maximize the learning from these activities it is essential that the learners receive feedback on their performance, and this needs observation of the activities, usually with the help of observational instruments. These are as much training aids when used with activities as the OHP, flipchart, etc are to input sessions. The range of such instruments is extensive, most types of activity requiring their own special type of instrument. Some of the ones in common use include:

- FREE OBSERVATION
- SELF-REPORTING
- TASK OBSERVATION
- PROCESS ANALYSIS
- INTERACTIVE
    BEHAVIOUR ANALYSIS
- VIDEO RECORDING

FREE OBSERVATION

This is the simplest form of observation, although in most cases far from the most effective. During an activity the participants, including any external observers, take as much notice as possible of the activity process, what is said and what is done, without any directive brief. At the end of the activity these observations are shared and summarized so that the learning points can be extracted. Hopefully, if the group of learners is aware, most of the learning points will emerge, but more usually a number of points, even important ones, are omitted. If this happens the trainer is required to become involved and comment on these – this can have a detrimental effect if the learners object to this intervention.

However, if the activity is introduced as a spontaneous support to the learning, free observation may be the only approach and obviously will be better than none at all.

SELF-REPORTING

In many ways this is similar to free observation, in that the observation is fairly free ranging and depends on the awareness (self-awareness in this case) of the learners. However, in this case, the learners are provided with a questionnaire that seeks their views on how they felt they performed in various aspects of the activity.

It can be useful in some cases to issue this questionnaire at the start of the activity to give the learners some indication of what they should be looking for while they are performing the activity. Otherwise, the questionnaires are handed out at the end of the activity and sufficient time given for the learners to recall their actions and feelings before recording these. Usually this recording is followed by a full group discussion, during which the learners share their views and encourage comments on their views by other members of the group. The end result of this discussion is a summary of the learning points that emerged from the activity and plans can be made for future action. This process reflects the learning cycle suggested by Kolb, and Honey and Mumford (see Chapter 1) in that it:

- provides an experience that can be reflected on (completing the questionnaire)
- gives the opportunity for analysing and theorizing about the experience (the discussion)

■ enables planning for future pragmatic action (in the discussion but also as a result of self-analysis).

This approach can be used successfully with activities such as meetings (both membership and leadership), problem-solving activities (again both membership and leadership), role plays, etc, the questions being designed with the particular activity in mind. An example of this type of questionnaire used by the chairperson or leader of a practice meeting is shown in Figure 11.1. The members of the meeting would have their own self-awareness questionnaire with questions relating to membership rather than leadership.

You have just completed chairing a meeting with your group. Please now try to recall what happened during the meeting, particularly your actions that made it either a success or something less than you would have wanted. You have xx minutes to think about this and record your thoughts, after which we shall hold a group discussion. The other members of the group have been given a questionnaire relating to their behaviour in the meeting.

1. How well did you feel you understood the objectives of the meeting?
2. How well did you feel you explained the objectives to the members?
3. Did you have to organize the meeting in any particular way, and how did you do this?
4. To what extent did you seek and use existing expertise from the membership?
5. How well did you enable *all* members to have the opportunity to express their views?
6. To what extent did you bring in members, particularly the quieter ones?
7. How well did you control the interactions between the members?
8. Which leadership style did you use? Was this effective? Was it the most effective one?
9. What did you do that you felt was particularly helpful?
10. What did you do that you felt was not so helpful?
    (a) How did you go about identifying the problems?
    (b) How did you manage to obtain alternative proposals for the solution?
    (c) How did you identify and have agreed the solution or final proposal?
    (d) To what extent did you summarize during the meeting?

On a scale of 1 (well) to 10 (badly), how did you feel you led the meeting? Record anything else in addition that you feel is relevant.

Figure 11.1 *An example self-awareness questionnaire*

If the training programme is principally concerned with meeting leadership skills the discussion might concentrate on the views of the leader on their leadership, the members giving feedback by commenting on these views, and relating these to their own activities.

TASK OBSERVATION

Self-awareness reporting is valuable, in that it involves the learners to a considerable extent in self-inspection, and is frequently a much more acceptable method of receiving feedback than from others – I will accept telling myself that I am a fool much more than if Fred told me! However, there is a truism that the observer sees more than the participant. As far as observable actions and behaviours are concerned this is more than a truism and, of course, these are principally the aspects on which we are able to give feedback. Recalling Johari, there will always be areas about which we are not aware.

If we introduce an observation instrument the observation and subsequent feedback will tend to be more objective, although subjectivity can rarely be avoided completely. The instrument will give guidelines to the observers on aspects and areas of the task and process that they should be looking out for – these will obviously be based mainly on the learning points of the event, as everything cannot be covered.

The self-awareness questionnaire described above can be developed into an observer's instrument by relating the questions to the person observed for both observation and feedback. Let us take again the example of the practice meeting with a leader and participating members where the emphasis is on leadership skills. This might be in a training programme where all the members will have the opportunity of taking the leader role and receiving feedback.

At the end of the meeting the leader can be given a slightly modified copy of the self-awareness questionnaire shown in Figure 11.1 to complete. The members, instead of completing a questionnaire on their own behaviour, would complete a questionnaire similar to that being self-completed by the leader, in this case commenting on how they saw his or her actions. The leader questionnaire would now appear as in Figure 11.2 and that for the members as in Figure 11.3.

Following completion of the questionnaires the trainer might lead a discussion based on how the skills of the leader were seen, by the leader him or herself, by the members and, as a final summary and top-up of points not mentioned, by the trainer. The feedback should be viewed as supportively critical rather than destructive – in practice this support usually occurs as the members know that their turn is still to come!

You have just completed chairing a meeting with your group. Please now try to recall what happened during the meeting, particularly your actions that made it either a success or something less than you would have wanted. You have xx minutes to think about this and record your thoughts, after which we shall hold a group discussion. The other members of the group have been given a questionnaire on which to record their views about your behaviour during the meeting.

1. How well did you feel you understood the objectives of the meeting?
2. How well did you feel you explained the objectives to the members?
3. Did you have to organize the meeting in any particular way and, if so, how did you do this?
4. To what extent did you seek and use existing expertise from the membership?
5. How well did you enable all members to have the opportunity to express their views?
6. To what extent did you bring in members, particularly the quieter ones?
7. How well did you control the interactions between the members?
8. Which leadership style did you use? Was this effective? Was it the most effective one?
9. What did you do that you felt was particularly helpful?
10. What did you do that you felt was not so helpful?
    (a) How did you go about identifying the problems?
    (b) How did you manage to obtain alternative proposals for the solution?
    (c) How did you identify and have agreed the solution or final proposal?
    (d) To what extent did you summarize during the meeting?

On a scale of 1 (well) to 10 (badly), how did you feel you led the meeting? On a similar scale, how do you think the members will rate your performance?
Record anything else in addition that you feel is relevant.

Figure 11.2 *An example, modified, leader's self-awareness questionnaire*

PROCESS ANALYSIS

The questionnaires in Figures 11.2 and 11.3 can be used in more extended observation for feedback purposes when it is possible to use observers external to the activity. These will usually be members taken

You have just completed a practice with your group with one of the group taking the part of the meeting leader. Please now try to recall what happened during the meeting, particularly the leader's actions that made it either a success or something less than you would have wanted. You have xx minutes to think about this and record your thoughts, after which we shall hold a group discussion. The other members of the group have been given a similar questionnaire on which to record their views of the meeting leadership.

1. How well did the leader help you to understand the objectives of the meeting?
2. Was the meeting organized in any particular way and, if so, how was this done?
3. To what extent did the leader seek and use existing expertise from the membership?
4. How well did the leader enable all members to have the opportunity to express their views?
5. To what extent did the leader bring in members, particularly the quieter ones?
6. How well were interactions between the members controlled?
7. Which leadership style was used? Was this effective? Was it the most effective one?
8. What did the leader do that you felt was particularly helpful?
9. What did the leader do that you felt was not so helpful?
   (a) How did the leader go about helping the members to identify the problems?
   (b) How well did the leader manage to seek alternative proposals for the solution?
   (c) How was the solution or final proposal agreed?
   (d) To what extent did the leader summarize during the meeting?

On a scale of 1 (well) to 5 (badly), how did you feel the leader led the meeting?
Record anything else in addition that you feel is relevant.

Figure 11.3 *An example observation questionnaire for members*

from the learning group and allocated the observer task for that activity: in the same way that leadership roles will progress through the group, so will the observer roles, so that everybody in the group has the opportunity of being in both roles at some stage during the programme.

Because the observers are not taking part in the activity, if necessary the observation guide can be more extensive than the self-awareness version, all the learning points for the activity being covered. There is, however, the temptation to ask the observers to look for a much larger number of items, often many more than necessary. This temptation can be resisted by concentrating on the activity's learning points and, if this list is too extensive, tasks can be shared between the observers.

The learning points will obviously vary with the activity and programme objectives. They can be task related, in which application of the techniques and methods of the skill being learned are examined: this can be a progressive process as the skills unfold with each input session followed by a practical activity to practise the skills. Or, in a social or interactive skills programme, behaviour would be the area of skills under scrutiny. In some cases observation might be of both task and behaviour, and in such cases a sharing of observational areas among several observers is desirable.

For all these different situations there are many different forms of observation instrument that are usually described in the source texts for the particular skills.

Task skills

Instruments for task observation, as commented above, will vary considerably depending on the skills covered by the activity or programme. One example of such an observation guide might be concerned with a presentation skills programme, with each learner taking turns at making a presentation. Specific observers might be allocated for these presentations, their eventual feedback being supported by the remainder of the 'audience' and the trainer. The instrument itself can require simple text comments, score ratings, or a mixture of both, the latter, in my experience, being the most useful in eventual feedback.

Figure 11.4 suggests the basic format for an observation sheet of this kind, additional questions being included according to the range of learning to be observed. If scoring is used there must be insistence on supporting comments, as simple scoring is too easy to record without in-depth consideration.

The demands placed on the observers can be wider than in the example quoted below, broad headings giving the observers considerable latitude in what they record, although within the limits of the learning. Figure 11.5 suggests such an observation guide for a team skills practice.

PRESENTATION OBSERVATION SHEET

Observe the presenter and record as many comments as you can about all aspects of their presentation. For each aspect give a score rating of 6 (very good or very well done) to 1 (poor or poorly done), ringing the relevant score, and also supporting this score with comments and examples.

HOW WELL DID THE PRESENTER INTRODUCE
THE PRESENTATION?   6 5 4 3 2 1
Comments:
WAS ANY IMPACT METHOD USED TO START THE
PRESENTATION AND HOW EFFECTIVE WAS THIS?   6 5 4 3 2 1
Comments:
HOW WELL DID THE PRESENTER DESCRIBE
QUESTIONING METHODS?   6 5 4 3 2 1
HOW WELL DID THE PRESENTER DESCRIBE
HOW THE PRESENTATION WOULD BE
STRUCTURED?   6 5 4 3 2 1
TO WHAT EXTENT DID THE PRESENTER FOLLOW
THE ANNOUNCED STRUCTURE?   6 5 4 3 2 1
TO WHAT EXTENT WAS THE PRESENTER
SUCCESSFUL IN PUTTING OVER THE REQUIRED
POINTS OF THE PRESENTATION?   6 5 4 3 2 1
etc

Figure 11.4 *Part example of task observation sheet*

Task and process skills

If observation of both the task practice and the behavioural skills involved is required for feedback following an event, then either more extensive observation sheets can be introduced or different observers can be allocated to look at various aspects. The sheets described in Figures 11.4 and 11.5 can be modified for these purposes by simply adding more, relevant questions on which the observers would need to comment.

When this wide range of observation is required very detailed observation guide sheets can be introduced, particularly when the observers are quite skilled, *au fait* with the process, and there will be time available for a detailed examination of what happened during the activity. An example of this type of guide is shown in Figure 11.6, when the detailed process of an activity needs to be observed.

TEAM LEADER OBSERVATION

ON THIS SHEET RECORD AS MANY COMMENTS AS POSSIBLE ABOUT WHAT YOU OBSERVE DURING THE TEAM PRACTICE ACTIVITY AND BE PREPARED TO PRESENT YOUR FINDINGS AT THE END OF THE ACTIVITY.

START OF THE EVENT. How and how well did the leader introduce the team event and get it started? Did the leader use any particular techniques for this purpose? How well did the leader organize the team? Were roles allocated and, if so, how was this done? Did the leader determine specific experience and expertise among the team, relevant to the activity?

DURING THE EVENT. To what extent did the leader influence the progress or otherwise of the activity? What did the leader do specifically to help the process? What did the leader do specifically to hinder the process? How well did the leader involve all members of the team? How well did the leader seek proposals and possible solutions? How well and by which method did the leader guide the team to a decision? Were these decisions made by the leader or the group?

END OF THE EVENT. Did the leader summarize the event and how well was this done? How and how well did the leader terminate the event?

Figure 11.5   *Example of broad task observation sheet*

The fishbowl

Whether the observations being made of a group relate to task or behaviour, or both, there are several specific techniques available to make observation a more effective training and learning aid. One of these is known as the Fishbowl technique, the name reflecting the observation of goldfish in a bowl.

The technique can be used when the learning group is divided into two, one half to be the activity (for example, a discussion or problem-solving activity) participants, the other half to be the observers. The participants, having been briefed, are seated in a circle ready to start their activity. The observers are seated in a circle outside the participants' circle and each observer is allocated a participant to observe, as shown in Figure 11.7. Observation sheets or free observation can be used, depending on the nature of the activity and the experience of the observers. As the event progresses the observers will take notes about what their allocated participant is saying or not saying, doing or not doing, whether they are helping or hindering, and so on.

ACTIVITY OBSERVATION SHEET

THIS OBSERVATION SHEET IS DIVIDED INTO TIME SECTIONS OF TWO
MINUTES. RECORD AS THE ACTIVITY PROGRESSES WHAT IS
HAPPENING AT THESE INTERVALS IN TERMS OF BOTH THE TASK AND
THE INTERACTIVE PROCESSES. BE PREPARED TO DISCUSS YOUR
OBSERVATIONS FOLLOWING THE EVENT.

Minutes   Comments

Start

2

4

6

8

10

12

14

16

18

20

End

Figure 11.6 *Example of a detailed, time-bounded observation sheet*

At the end of the event the observers give the participants feedback about their performance, either on a one-to-one basis or the full group, or using both these approaches. Commonly, after the feedback session, the participant/observer roles are reversed and the process is repeated so that all the learners eventually receive feedback on their group performances.

INTERACTIVE BEHAVIOUR ANALYSIS

One of the most frequently used training aids in observation is some form of activity analysis, particularly where the analysis is concerned with the frequency of behaviour in a group. There are several approaches to this observation, with increasing complexity.

OBSERVER

PARTICIPANT

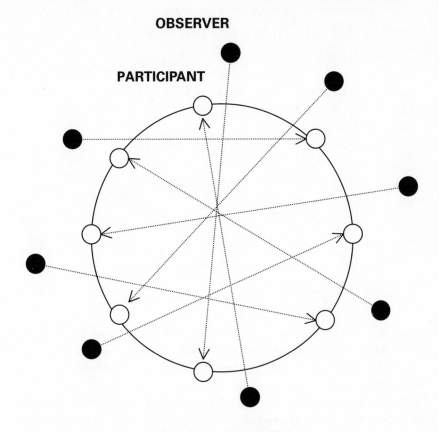

Figure 11.7 *The Fishbowl*

SIMPLE CONTRIBUTION SCORING

This is probably the simplest form of contribution incidence scoring and is useful, when working with a large group, in identifying quantitatively who are the high, medium and low contributors to the activity. This information can then be used to encourage the modification of the behaviours of certain members.

The names of the participants are entered on a sheet of paper, preferably in the order in which they are seated for ease of identification, and each time a participant makes a contribution (ie speaks) a stroke or other mark is made alongside their name. At the end of the event there will be a set of strokes against each member's name indicating how many contributions they made during the event. Figure 11.8 shows an example of this type of recording aid.

In this example the recording aid shows a wide variance in the contribution level of the participating members. This is what one would

Fred	||||| ||||| ||||| ||||| ||||| ||||| |||||		
																				49
Jean														7
Harry	|||							3
Sally																										21
Mary	||||| ||||| ||||| ||||| ||||| ||||| |||||		
																	45
Rita									1
George																												23
Ahmed	|||||							5
Richard																															27
Kir	|||							3
Louise																				13
TOTAL									197

Figure 11.8 *Simple contribution scoring*

expect in a heterogeneous group, but examination shows that some of the variations are greater than one would desire in a learning group.

The record does little more than quantify the contributions in bare numerical terms, but it raises questions for consideration and discussion. For example, why did Rita make only one contribution and Kir and Harry only three each, whereas Fred and Mary made 94 contributions between them, almost half the total contributions of the group. Were Rita, Kir and Harry as quiet as the record shows? Why did they not contribute more? Was it because Fred and Mary, and to some extent Sally, George and Richard did so much talking that they had no chance to enter the discussion?

In the same way, why were Fred and Mary allowed to get away with dominating the discussion to such an extent – was one of them in fact the leader (not a very effective one)?

The percentage of each person's contributions can also be calculated for comparisons in real terms with the contribution rates in other events, particularly if, after discussion of these results, behaviour modification plans are made.

This type of recording only shows the number of contributions, not their length, nature and value to the discussion. Fred's contributions may have been principally unimportant one-worders, and Rita's single contribution may have been the most important one of the event – if this was indeed the case, why was she not encouraged to contribute more? The record obviously raises many questions, but to obtain the other type of information other forms of observation are necessary.

Variations

One practical variation from the format shown in Figure 11.8, intended to make numerical identification easier, is, instead of single strokes, sets of five can be banded together in what are known as 'five-barred gates':

卌

A rather more radical variation is to use a sequential recording that adds another element to the analytical possibilities. In this case, the initials of the contributors are used (A, R, K, F etc) and entered as each person speaks so that the sequence of contribution as well as the frequency can be analysed:

A, R, F, K, F, R, F, M, F, R, F, RA (Rita), etc

One of the details that this analysis will show is that not only is Fred a high contributor (as we saw in the simple record), but that he is also a highly reactive contributor, needing to enter the discussion after everybody else's comments.

A rather more difficult record to complete, albeit one that extends the amount of information to be obtained, is to link the sequencing with the length of the contribution. It is, with practice, relatively easy to judge intervals of ten seconds, so instead of just entering the contributor's initial, it is repeated every ten seconds that the contribution lasts.

AAA, RRRRRRRR, F, KK, F, RRRRRRRRRR, F, MMMM,
F, RRRRR, F, RARARARARARARAR (Rita), etc

DIRECTIONAL SOCIOGRAMS

On occasions an observation of a group at work needs to have different objectives than simply recording the number or frequency of the contributions. We can record the way in which the group discussion flows between the members of the group, in addition to the number of contributions and some other aspects of communication. Such recording methods are known as sociograms.

In this case we start with a sheet paper on which circles or other positional marks represent the members of the group in their relative seating positions. It is useful, before the interaction, to join all the circles to each other with lines representing the way in which they *could* communicate with each other. Short lines emerging from each circle towards the outside of the group can be used to show contributions made to the group as a whole rather than to individual members. This initial sociogram is shown in Figure 11.9.

Whenever a member of the group speaks the observer will identify the person to whom the contribution is made and place a mark on the line joining the two people. If the contribution is made generally to the group as a whole, the mark is placed on the line directed outwards. The contribution marks can be simple strokes across the line, Xs, or arrows, and a different mark can be used to show when one member interrupts another.

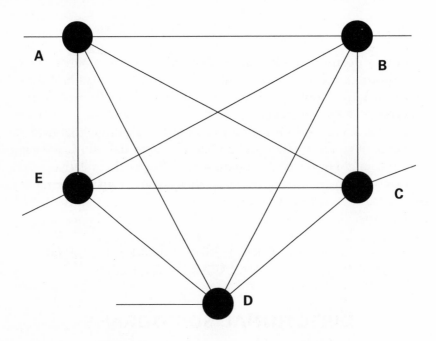

Figure 11.9 *Initial directional sociogram*

In Figure 11.10 arrows are shown for contributions and a stroke across the line for an interruption. The figure after the letter shows the number of contributions (including interruptions) made by that individual.

The sociogram shows that in this 'discussion' there were actually four discussions taking place, the group being divided into sub-groups. Member D had to hold a meeting on his own, his contributions being

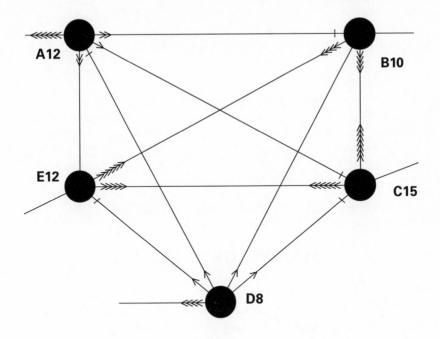

Figure 11.10   *Directional sociogram*

mainly to the group as a whole. He did speak to all the members, but everybody interrupted him! Consequently he had to broadcast his views to the group hoping that someone would react to him – nobody did! Members B, C and E had a discussion almost exclusive to themselves, B and C interrupting A (the chairperson) when she tried to speak to them. A tried contacting most of the members but with minimal success, and like D was reduced to making comments to the group, most of which appear to have been ignored.

The directional sociogram is a powerful training aid to identify a range of information in a group of activity. One disadvantage can be that, while the observer is completing the record, it will be difficult for him or her to record other forms of observation. This is not impossible, particularly for a skilled observer, but it may be necessary for more than one observer to be used.

It is possible to analyse the group interaction directly from the sociogram, but some analysts prefer to transfer the information to a matrix. Using the sociogram data from Figure 11.10 this would produce a matrix as shown in Figure 11.11, the bracketed figures representing the interruptions.

To:	A	B	C	D	E	F	G	GROUP	TOTAL
From:									
A	–	2	1	–	–	1	2	9	15
B	(1)	–	5	–	–	–	1	1	8
C	(1)	5	–	(1)	1	1	1	1	11
D	–	–	1	–	1	–	–	4	6
E	–	–	–	(1)	–	5	4	–	10

Figure 11.11 *Directional sociogram data in matrix form*

BEHAVIOUR ANALYSIS

Many of the observation training and learning aids considered so far have been concerned with either the skills concerned or the process of the event. A substantial element in many training programmes is concerned with the people involved and their behavioural characteristics. Particularly in interactive skills programmes there is an emphasis on the behavioural aspects of the learners, their interrelational effects and the ways in which these behaviours might be modified, if necessary. In order to provide the learners with information about themselves in these areas it is necessary to observe them in a variety of situations and analyse the behaviour patterns demonstrated.

The training aids used to provide this type of information are described as interaction or behaviour analyses. The introduction of this type of analysis is attributed to R F Bales (1950) with his Interaction Process Analysis, which sought to relate behaviour categories to identifiable problem areas in the task and socio-emotional aspects. However, most of the interaction analysis instruments that followed from Bales are more useful for behavioural research than practical training and development. A major exception is the behaviour analysis instrument introduced by Neil Rackham, Terry Morgan, Peter Honey and others, which they called Behaviour Analysis (BA). From the basis of the analysis observational instruments can be produced with which behaviours can be observed and recorded for eventual analysis, feedback and modification. This basis is strictly controlled within the model, a number of criteria having to be followed in deciding how to select and describe the categories of behaviour shown by people. Reference should be made to the original works for definitive information on these bases.

Behaviour categories

More important from the practical point of view is the range of behaviour categories that can be used in observation instruments for different situations. The behaviour categories that are commonly used in BA when the behaviour of people in groups is being observed are as follows.

Proposing. A behaviour that puts forward a proposal as a statement and as a bid for a new idea or course of action. Eg 'I propose that we send this communication.'

Suggesting. Putting forward a proposal in a less dogmatic manner, in the form of a question rather than as a statement. Eg 'How does everybody feel about the idea of sending this communication?'

Building. A supportive proposal that extends or develops a proposal made by another person and that enhances the original proposal. Eg 'Yes, and we could also send the other information we discussed.'

Seeking information, opinions, feelings. Asking questions to elicit information from others. Eg 'What does anybody know about the new machinery?'

Seeking ideas. Questioning others about proposals or suggestions they might wish to make. Eg 'Has anyone any ideas how we might go ahead with this?'

Giving information, views, opinions, feelings. Making statements from a personal knowledge or feelings base, but without going to the extent of making a proposal. Eg 'When I was at so-and-so the way that it was done was . . .'

Disagreeing. Simply stating disagreement with the views of others without giving reasons for this attitude. Eg 'No, I can't go along with that' or simply 'No, I disagree!'

Disagreeing with reasons. Disagreeing with another's views, but in a more positive manner by stating the reasons for disagreement. Eg 'Right, that sounds like a good idea, but I don't think it would work here because . . .'

Supporting. A conscious or direct declaration of support for another person or their views. Eg 'Yes, I'll go along with that. It seems to be a good idea.'

Testing understanding. A behaviour that attempts to check whether a contribution made by another has been understood. Eg 'If I've got it right, what you are saying is . . .'

Summarizing. A statement that collects in a compact form the content of discussions and decisions made to that stage of the event or in a previous event. Eg 'What we have decided in this meeting covers three areas. First, we decided that we should . . .'

Open. This is a behaviour in which the speaker accepts or admits an error or omission, or apologizes for their actions. Eg 'Yes, I should have done that' or even, simply, 'Sorry.'

Blocking. A contribution that does nothing to progress the discussion and offers no alternative proposal for action. It then requires a positive contribution by someone else. Eg 'Oh we're just going round in circles.'

Attacking. A statement made to another person that has overt value judgements on the other or contains emotive overtones. Eg 'I might have expected *you* to say something like that!'

Bringing in. A direct and positive attempt to involve another person. Usually linked with a question, and counts as two behaviours. Eg 'What do you think about that, *Mary*?'

Shutting out. A behaviour that excludes, or attempts to exclude others' contributions, by interrupting them, contributing when someone brought in hasn't yet spoken, or when two or more participants engage in side discussions outside the main discussion.

GROUP BEHAVIOUR ANALYSIS PRACTICE

BA is carried out by an observer or analyst making a record of the group in action, identifying the categories of the behaviours exhibited by all the members during the activity. This is performed by the making of a stroke or mark on a Behaviour Analysis sheet, in a rather similar way to the simple contribution scoring method, but to a much more in-depth degree.

Figure 11.12 gives an example of a group BA sheet containing vertical columns for each participant and 16 horizontal rows for the categories included in the observation – in this case the ones described above. The strokes have been totalled and entered as the number of contributions.

A skilled and experienced BA observer is required to record the contributions of a group of people against 16 categories, as it is necessary to:

■ identify the person who spoke
■ identify the category of the contribution
■ enter the scoring stroke in the appropriate space.

Under many conditions this is not too difficult for the experienced analyst, although problems do arise when the contributions are being

BEHAVIOUR ANALYSIS: ACTIVITY.......................

Period of observation ....

	John	Mike	Sally	Jean	Ralph	Mary	Totals
Proposing	9	15		2	15	4	45
Suggesting			2				2
Building	1					2	3
Seeking ideas	5			1	1		7
Seeking information	16	6	1	5	15	19	62
Giving information	12	22	12	14	14	25	99
Disagreeing		6	2			4	12
Disagreeing with reasons	3		2		3		8
Supporting	6			8		10	24
Testing understanding	2						2
Summarizing	7					1	8
Open	1					1	2
Blocking		6			6		12
Attacking		2			3		5
Bringing in	6		2	2			10
Interrupting	6	15	1	6	8	14	50
Totals	74	72	22	38	65	80	351

Figure 11.12   *A Behaviour Analysis sheet*

made thick and fast, particularly when there are attacks and interruptions being made. In most cases only one person at a time is speaking and this makes the task easier.

When the observer/analyst is less experienced or is drawn from the group the number of categories included must be reduced to make the task easier and more reliable. Obviously the more limited the number of categories observed the more limited will be the information recorded and available for analysis.

A reduced BA observation sheet

If the number of categories has to be reduced the ones still included should be those identified as more significant for that particular activity. For example, if a problem-solving group is to be observed, a shortened list of categories might consist of:

- Proposing
- Seeking ideas
- Seeking information
- Giving information
- Summarizing
- Interrupting
- Other behaviours.

The format of such a reduced BA sheet is shown in Figure 11.13. It is essential if the 'full' range of categories is not included to have one category, 'Other behaviours', to keep the record complete. I have found that it can be useful to divide this general category into '+ve (or helpful) behaviours' and '–ve (or unhelpful behaviours) without increasing the number of categories to too great an extent.

BEHAVIOUR ANALYSIS: ACTIVITY							
Period of observation							
	John	Mike	Sally	Jean	Ralph	Mary	Totals
Proposing	9	15		2	15	4	45
Seeking ideas	5			1	1		7
Seeking information	16	6	1	5	15	19	62
Giving information	12	22	12	14	14	25	99
Summarizing	7					1	8
Interrupting	6	15	1	6	8	14	50
Other +ve behaviours	11	4	8	5	2	8	38
Other –ve behaviours	8	10		5	10	9	42
Totals	74	72	22	38	65	80	351

Figure 11.13 *A reduced category BA sheet*

Selective BA observation

During a training needs identification exercise or during the training programme itself it may emerge that some behavioural aspect is causing the learners particular difficulty. Or new behaviours may be being introduced and it is necessary to give the learners the opportunity to practise these. In such cases a customized BA that concentrates on the selected behaviours can be used as the observational aid.

For example, there may be problems occurring in meetings at work or in a meetings training programme. The categories that might help in such a case could produce a BA sheet as shown in Figure 11.14 to examine the proposing behaviour of the meeting group.

BEHAVIOUR ANALYSIS: PROPOSING BEHAVIOUR Period of observation	
Procedure proposals	
Content proposals	
Suggestions	
Building proposals	
Directive proposals	
Caught proposals	
Lost proposals	
Rejected proposals	
Repeat proposals	
Testing understanding	
Summarizing proposals made	
Totals	

Figure 11.14 *Selective category BA*

Other BA observation

BA observation is not restricted to group working, and in fact the BA is not only invaluable as a training aid in, for example one-to-one interactions, but is easier to perform as there will be only two people to record. The categories used can be customized to the event, the emphasis in this case being on questioning techniques, as far as the interviewer is concerned. A suggested BA sheet for recording a practice counselling interview is shown in Figure 11.15. In cases such as this the number of categories is not critical because of the limited number of participants involved and the greater ease in observing fewer contributors.

BEHAVIOUR ANALYSIS: ACTIVITY......................			
Period of observation......................			
	Interviewer	Interviewee	Totals
Proposing/Suggesting			
Open questions			
Closed questions			
Multiple questions			
Leading questions			
Reflecting			
Giving information			
Disagreeing with reasons			
Disagreeing			
Testing understanding			
Summarizing			
Supporting			
Open			
Attacking			
Interrupting			
Totals			

Figure 11.15   *BA sheet for a one-to-one interaction*

The use of Fishbowl observation has been described earlier. A BA sheet similar to Figure 11.15, but with only one column for recording the contributions of the one participant being observed can be useful in these cases, supplemented by any other task observations necessary. The extra work involved here is simplified because the observer is concentrating on one participant only.

Non-verbal BA observation

BA is not only useful as a training aid for verbal behaviour. BA sheets for groups or one-to-one interactions can be constructed to record non-verbal signals in a similar format to those described for verbal interactions. In the group observation situation it would be too difficult a task for one observer to record both verbal and non-verbal contributions, but as suggested earlier separate tasks can be allocated to more than one observer. It is possible, although still not easy, for one observer to perform both tasks when observing a one-to-one interaction or in a Fishbowl observation.

One final benefit of BA, in addition to the provision of relatively accurate, quantitative and unbiased data for analysis, is its use as a listening training aid. There can be no doubt that when an observer has a BA sheet to complete as an activity or discussion proceeds, he or she must be listening very carefully to all the contributions in order to enter the records accurately.

12

Conclusion

THE NECESSARY STEPS

The preceding material describes and reproduces a number of resources for a wide range of training aids that are in common use nowadays in training and development. The descriptions include those aids, traditional and developing, that we immediately recognize within the genus 'aids', and also instruments and methods we do not immediately think of in the description. Whatever the format or nature of the aid you should remember that they are *aids*, whose purpose is to support and enhance other activities – trainer input sessions, training programmes, self-instruction packages, etc – so that improved learning might result. They should always be viewed in this light, and must not be allowed to become the training programme itself, or be relied on as training briefs. Remember Murphy and the likelihood (because many of the aids rely on electric and electronic equipment) that something could and probably will go wrong. If they are there to support you and problems arise, the main learning process can go ahead, albeit not quite as effectively, but certainly more so than if the session had to be abandoned because of power or equipment failure.

Training aids are tools to be used by the trainer, and in many cases the learner. It is most unlikely that any one programme will use all the possible aids, but you must be certain that you are using the most appropriate aid(s) for the situation. Now that the range of common aids has been covered, let us return to the process of selecting the most appropriate one(s). Some of the details necessary for selection were discussed in Chapter 2. This discussion suggested a selection process to be followed at your programme planning stage:

Questions to ask

- What am I trying to achieve in this session or presentation? What are its objectives?
- Can the session objectives be achieved without training aids?
- Even though the objectives can be achieved without aids, will learning be made easier and/or be improved if the verbal presentation is supported?
- Do the session objectives, content and style demand the support of training aids?
- Will training aids improve the presentation?
- Which aids will be the most appropriate?
- Are there other aids that might be more effective?
- How many will I need?
- Is it feasible to use the number on which I decide?
- How available are the resources?
- Have I the resources – time, staff support, finance – to produce or obtain the aids?

The foregoing descriptions of many of the training and learning aids currently available should put you in a position to make a considered, relevant and effective selection.

References and suggested reading

Baguley, Phil (1994) *Effective Communication for Modern Business*, 2nd edn, McGraw-Hill.

Bales, R F (1950) *Interaction Process Analysis*, Addison-Wesley.

Bell, Chris (1994) Using Training Aids, in John Prior (ed.) *Handbook of Training and Development*, 2nd edn), Gower.

Corder, Colin (1990) *Teaching Hard Teaching Soft*, Gower.

Dean, C and Whitlock, Q (1988) *A Handbook of Computer Based Training*, 2nd edn, Kogan Page.

Ellington, Henry and Race, Phil (1993) *Producing Teaching Materials: A Handbook for Teachers and Trainers*, 2nd edn, Kogan Page.

Flegg, David and McHale, Josephine (1991) *Selecting and Using Training Aids*, Kogan Page.

Flesch, R (1949) *The Art of Readable Writing*, Harper & Row.

Gunning, R (1952) *The Technique of Clear Writing*, Kogan Page.

Harrison, Nigel (1995) *Practical Instructional Design for Open Learning Materials*, 2nd edn: *A modular course covering open learning, computer-based training and multimedia*, McGraw-Hill.

Hodgson, Vivien and McConnell, David (1994) On-line Education and Development, in John Prior (ed.), *Handbook of Training and Development*, 2nd edn, Gower.

Honey, Peter (1988) *Face to Face*, 2nd edn, Gower.

Honey, Peter (1994) *Learning Log*, Peter Honey Publications.

Honey, Peter and Mumford, Alan (1992) *The Manual of Learning Styles*, Peter Honey.

Hottos, S (1993) *CD-I Designers Guide*, McGraw-Hill.

King, Graham (1993) various titles in the *Sunday Times* 14-booklet *One Hour Wordpower Series*. Mandarin Reference.

Kolb, David A (1984) *Learning Style Inventory (Experiential Learning Experience as a Source of Learning and Development)*, Prentice-Hall.

Luft, Joseph (1970) *Group Processes: An Introduction to Group Dynamics*, Mayfield Publishing.

Pinnington, Ashley (1992) *Using Video in Training and Education*, McGraw-Hill.

Race, Phil and Smith, Brenda (1995) *500 Tips for Trainers*, Kogan Page.

Rackham, Neil et al. (1971) *Developing Interactive Skills*, Wellens.

Rackham, Neil and Morgan, Terry (1977) *Behaviour Analysis in Training*, McGraw-Hill.

Rae, Leslie (1992) *A Guide to In-company Training Methods*, Gower.

Rae, Leslie (1994) *How to Design and Introduce Trainer Development Programmes*, Kogan Page.

Rae, Leslie (1997) *How to Measure Training Effectiveness*, 3rd edn, Gower.

Rae, Leslie (1995) *The Techniques of Training*, 3rd edn, Gower.

Rae, Leslie (1994) *The Trainer Development Programme*, Kogan Page.

Rae, Leslie (1996) *Using Activities in Training and Development*, Kogan Page.

Rae, Leslie (1997) *Using Presentations in Training and Development*, Kogan Page.

Stimson, Nancy (1991) *How to Write and Prepare Training Materials*, Kogan Page.

Townsend, John (1996) *The Trainer's Pocketbook*, 8th edn, Management Pocketbooks.

Wynn, Peter (1994) Computer-based Training, in John Prior (ed.) *Handbook of Training and Development*, 2nd edn, Gower.

Index

people as training aids 142–3
photographic slide projector
    (35mm) 103–106
  advantages 103, 106
  back projection 105–106
  disadvantages 103–104
  slide preparation 104–105
pre-recorded videos 117–22
  as the training session 117–20
    stages for using 118–120
  as a self-instruction resource
    121–2
  as a trigger 121–2
  during a training event
    120–21

Rackham, Neil 222

selection of training aids 20–30,
    231–2
  aid to selection 26–30
    cost 28–30
    how many to use 26–28
selection process 20–24
  characteristics 22
  most appropriate 21–2
  questions to ask 20–21
  relevance 23–4
  session objectives 21
sensory learning 4–7
  sense of sight 5–6
  sense of hearing 6
  sense of touch 6
  senses of smell and taste 7
simulations 203–205
  summary 204–205
  timing 204
  usage 203–204
specific techniques for chalk-
    boards and flipcharts 41–4
  collecting views from the
    learning group 44
  pre-preparation 42–3

providing a focus 43–4
second flipchart 44
support for trainer's
    presentations 44
uses 42
synchronized tape–slide
    presenters 112–15
  advantages 113
  disadvantages 113
  preparation of presentations
    114–5

T-chart 43
tape–slide presentations 112–15
training aids 17–30
  aid to clarity and conciseness
    19
  aid to matching aids to
    methods 24–5
  aid to selection 26–30
    cost 28–30
    how many to use 26–8
  available aids 20
  consistency and quality of
    thought 19
  greater impact 18
  recall reinforcement
  selection process 20–24
    characteristics 22
    most appropriate 21–2
    questions to ask 20–21
    relevance 23–4
    session objectives 21
  transparencies for the OHP
    68–72, 72–91
    computer preparation 72–91
      borders and frames 75–6
      chart forms 85–91
        bar charts 87–8
        line charts 88–91
        pie charts 85–7
      choice of lettering 73
      colour printing 81